The Truth About Social Work

Social Work Tutor

Dedications

The travel, time off from work and resources needed to gather these tales of social work would not have been possible if it wasn't for the support of those who pre-ordered copies of this book before it was even written. Thanks go to:

Carey Wachtel, Lee Allen, Catherine O'Callaghan, Sakera Sheth, Lindsay Giddings, Darren Knibbs, Daniel McCabe, Damon Haughton, Lennox Reid, Emma Bilson, Jacob Robson, Monique Haetzold, Mary Parah, Max Greenwood, Dawn Weare, Mary Cullen, Zoe Martin, Mickel Hollman, Chris Gibbon, Dan Newbolt, Rebecca Jones and Purple Social Care Consultancy Limited.

Your faith in me will not be forgotten and I can never thank you enough for giving me the support I needed to undertake this journey.

Special thanks go out to my official sponsors for their help in getting this book over the line and for allowing me the freedom to make this dream a reality:

Child Protection Training UK

Community Care

Liquid Personnel

Shanti Boafar of Ellis Ellly

Sharon Moseley of Team Twenty

Social Justice Solutions

It has been an honour to be associated with such prestigious organisations.

I also want to thank my wife for all that she has had to put up with
over the past year. It's hard living with a social worker at the best
of times, never knowing when they'll be home or what they'll have
gone through that day. It must be even harder living with one who
comes home from work then, after tea and putting the baby to bed,
sits at the kitchen table for hours on end; writing articles, poring
over research, working on his book and talking to fellow social
workers going through difficulties all over the world.

I couldn't have done this without you my love.

Finally, my daughter. You are the reason I strive so hard to make
the world a better place. Even if I'm sometimes not home in time to
read you a bedtime story, you are always on my mind.

Copyright

Printed in the United Kingdom

First edition published in 2017

ISBN 978-1-9998392-0-8

Social Work Tutor Publishing
Napier Court, Gander Lane, Barlborough,
Chesterfield, Derbyshire, England, S43 4PZ

www.socialworktutor.com

Contents

Introduction

How can the poem and the stink and the grating noise- the quality of light, the tone, the habit and the dream- be set down alive? When you collect marine animals, there are certain flat worms so delicate that they are almost impossible to capture whole, for they break and tatter under the touch. You must let them ooze and crawl of their own will on to a knife blade and then lift them gently into your bottle of sea water. And perhaps that might be the way to write this book- to open the page and to let the stories crawl in by themselves.

John Steinbeck (1945) Cannery Row

One lazy May afternoon in 1998, I was sat at the back of my English Literature class, talking with my friends about anything other than the subject we were supposed to be studying at the time. Like many young men with a slight gift for learning, I was choosing to cruise through my secondary education with the bare minimum of effort instead of applying myself. The notion of deferred gratification had not dawned on me at the age of fourteen, and indeed would not do so until many years later.

I thought I was being clever at the time and had somehow discovered a trick to 'win' at life, posting in my education with little effort and freeing up time in school to joke around with my friends.

My English Teacher, Mr Bowley, had loftier ambitions for me than I did for myself and at the end of class he asked me to stay behind. Bracing myself for another dressing down for disrupting the rest of the class, he instead took a different track and placed Of Mice and Men by John Steinbeck into my hands. 'You think you're smarter than the rest of the class' he told me 'now go ahead and prove it'. Accompanying the tatty dog-eared schools' edition of Steinbeck's book was a photocopied sheet of questions that the pupils in the class two years above me were using to prepare for their pending GCSE exams.

Education, and indeed life in general, seems so linear when you're that age and everything appears to be out of reach. All the things you want to do are forbidden because you're too young. All the riches, rewards and freedoms of adult life seem so exotic because you can't have them. The rigid class structures of compulsory education indoctrinate you into a way of prescribed education that says you're not ready for the next stage yet. Blinkered by this way of thinking, I saw his request as extra homework, a punishment, or a way to knock me down a peg or two. I'd flunk the task in spectacular style and it would be a reminder that I wasn't nearly half as clever as I thought I was, letting me know that I needed to pay more attention in class.

I got home with the intention of skimming over the first few pages just so I could embed my narrow-minded view that Mr Bowley was being a total dick to me (those were the kind of views I had and kind of words I used at fourteen), before going out to play football and spout this view out to my older friends who likely had a similarly disdainful view of sixty-year-old American literature.

Four hours later, having eaten tea in my bedroom, I'd read through the book in one sitting. That evening changed everything for me and was the start of a journey spanning two decades. A journey that finds you reading this book right now.

Steinbeck showed me that there is magic and wonder to be found in every walk of life. You don't have to be rich, pretty, privileged or lucky to make the most of the world around you. He took the tales of normal everyday working-class people, just like me and my Dad (who was working full-time as a coalman while at the same time bringing me up as a single parent) and made them seem special. George and Lenny were just two working class guys with a simple dream, yet their story had more of an impact on me than anything I'd read in grand fantasy tales by CS Lewis or Tolkien when I was younger and still reading every night.

What I had once thought of as a punishment by Mr Bowley turned out to be one of the defining moments of my life. The love of Steinbeck that he instilled in me led me to Woody Guthrie, to Springsteen, to the Labour movement, to campaigning, to unions and eventually to social work. It also sparked my passion for writing about the truth as it is experienced by everyday people. It gave me the belief that writing isn't a closed shop- only open to those with a certain level of experience, qualifications or prestige- but is a medium that anyone can use to shine a light on their way of seeing the world.

As I set out to write this book, to achieve my lofty ambition of telling the tale of modern social work, I had little idea about how I would capture the essence of the profession in between two covers of a book. The blogs that I write and publish every day can capture the zeitgeist of our professional world at any given time because they are a snapshot of what is happening at that moment. If they fade out or become irrelevant after a few days it doesn't matter because they aren't built to last. A book is a very different beast though as these words are more tangible. They are set down on paper for eternity. I knew that the stories I captured here must be meaningful and tell a tale far more important than my own.

Searching for how I would go about writing this book, I found Stein-beck's prologue to Cannery Row coming back to me… perhaps that might be the way to write this book-to open the page and to let the stories crawl in by themselves.

I have spent a year speaking to people connected to the social work profession from all over the world and letting their stories crawl into this book by themselves. I had no agenda to push, no narrative of my own to spin and no political or business interests swaying my work. I simply approached people who had a story to tell and asked them if they'd let me capture them.

There are close to a hundred people I spoke to over the course of writing this book and I wish I could have captured all their tales. Some stories were too sad to tell as the grief of those affected was still too much to bear. Other interviews I decided to pull at the last minute because they were controversial and risked overshadow-ing the rest of this book. Many more people were just not ready to have their take on social work captured for prosperity at this moment in time. Their stories will remain stored on the two hun-dred hours of voice recordings I have on file and in the notebooks collecting dust in my attic. Perhaps they will come out again when they need to be heard.

Whilst I spoke to people from all over the globe in the process of gathering the true essence of what it means to be a social worker in this day and age, most of the stories making it into the book have come from those closer to home. Even if your country isn't represented in these pages, I hope you find that the stories I've set down are universal in their nature and you find affinity with what you read (as a side note, my North American friends can look for-ward to my next book *Fifty States of Social Work* which focuses entirely on your nation).

In seeking to 'let the stories crawl in by themselves', I struggled with distilling epic tales of social work into words, let alone into short enough chapters that I could fit twenty of them into a book. There are people's lives that I could have made a trilogy of books out of on their own. I wrote, rewrote and edited many of these chapters more times than I care to admit. I agonised over whether I should write them in the first person, third person or simply ask people to write their own views and give me permission to make some minor edits. In the end, I did all of those things.

Some chapters are traditional interviews in the long-form style, others are biographical accounts that I've crafted from extensive interviews and some are short pieces created by the subjects themselves. I have tried to select formats that I believe best suit the humans at the heart of the matter and that do their stories justice. The only general rule I have followed is to stagger chapters between shorter and longer pieces of writing.

What I have committed to paper is a collection of stories from people who I believe give us all something to think about. Their tales might not always be the cheeriest and their views might not always find parity with your own, but I trust that you find their experiences interesting, insightful and, most importantly, a true reflection of social work.

SWT

Chapter One: The social work stand ups

It's a cold, dark, wet and windy night in mid-December when I arrive in Preston, Lancashire.

After having to drive over the back of the north Pennines and down through the Lake District to get here, a journey of more than three hours from my home, I'm not in the most jovial of moods by the time I catch Jim and Deb walking into the restaurant we'd agreed to meet at before their gig tonight. I once dated a girl from Preston who broke my heart, cheating on me with a co-star in her university musical society's performance of *The Witches of Eastwick.* The memory of the two of them engaged in an intensely acted out kiss on stage, as me and her parents watched from the front row, is making me even grumpier than the drive already has.

But my mood is lifted as soon as Jim walks over to me and, instead of taking me by the hand that I'd extended, gives me a hug.

His eyes sparkle with enthusiasm, his mouth is wide with a truly happy smile and he comes across as genuinely pleased that I've made the journey down to see him and Deb tonight. 'No, the pleasure is all mine' I tell him as I respond to him thanking me for making the trip. And the pleasure really is all mine because I'd heard from many of my social work colleagues how funny their routine was and I can't wait to see it for myself.

Jim and Deb are an unlikely pairing and their background reads like the beginning of a joke- *"Did you hear the one about the social worker from Northern Ireland, the social worker from Australia and their plan to go into stand-up comedy?"*

It is the back story to how they got into comedy and paired up that intrigues me most (after all, how many social work comedians has anyone ever heard of before?) and, once we engage in some small talk and order food, I fire straight in and ask them how they came to be where they are now.

Jim begins by telling me how he'd always been someone who'd tried to look on the bright side of things and, where possible, would find humour wherever he could in his life. Although he doesn't use the word itself, I can't help but find myself thinking of the famous Irish 'craic' and seeing how Jim personifies this jovial approach to life as he talks of his outlook on the world.

A fan of comedy from an early age, Jim would regularly attend local open mic stand up nights when training in different cities throughout the United Kingdom; watching a range of comedians who were brave enough to get up and do their bit in front of others. After watching a succession of unimpressive amateur performers doing routines night after night, he had a recurring thought that 'I'd love to do that' and eventually built that thought into action. As Jim is telling me about his inspiration to take to the stage himself I think that, if I was a comedian myself, I should really have made a joke about precontemplation, contemplation, preparation, action and maintenance there. I'm not a comedian so I leave the jokes to the professionals but make a note that this witty observation should find itself into my writing instead, a medium I'm far more comfortable with.

16

He had the gift of natural timing, he had a well-lived life to draw upon for material and he had a social workers' gift of being good with people, so why not give it a go?

Unlike Jim's gradual calling to the microphone, Deb's decision to tread the pioneering path of the social work stand up came as more of a 'eureka' moment. She describes to me how she was in a meeting with her social work team members in Northern Ireland and discussing the possibility of holding a gathering outside of work. Like most social workers, the long hours and culture of individualism within the workplace left them with little time to bond, so they were thinking about remedying this with a social event tied to an awards evening that wasn't just based around a leaving party or Christmas.

Bandying around ideas for the event, Deb had a sudden urge to shout out "I'll do a stand-up routine".

With no experience of performing comedy before, or any prior urge to take up the mic, she had just blurted out a commitment to stand up in front of a room full of colleagues and do her thing. Half expecting to be shot down in flames due to how ludicrous the idea seemed, her plan gained traction and she walked away from the meeting with a promise to entertain her fellow social workers with a stand-up routine.

"I walked out of there with no idea how I was going to pull it off, but determined that I was going to manage it" she tells me when recalling a moment of inspiration that was to change the rest of her life. I comment that pulling off miracles is normal for a social worker and Deb smiles about her own efforts to pull a rabbit out of a hat.

For the next three months, she worked every day on pulling together the material needed to put on a comedy routine. With a young family at home and the never-ending demands of a social work job to contend with, it was her evenings and weekends that bore the brunt of her writing time; often working into the early hours to hone the raw material of her daily observations into jokes and anecdotes that would come across well to a crowd.

"The good thing about being a social worker is that we never run out of things to talk about!" Deb tells me as I ask how she went about putting her routine together. She would carry a small notebook around with her and, as soon as inspiration arose, would quickly write down an observation or comment that might eventually find its way into her routine.

Unlike Billy Connolly or Louis CK, Deb didn't have an agent to promote her show or push tickets on her behalf. This meant that, alongside the work to generate her material, she was having to take on all promotional duties as well. Looking back on the moment of inspiration that took hold of her in the team meeting, perhaps she would have held back had she realised the effort that goes into putting on a stand-up show. From the audiences' perspective, it might look like an hour of somebody telling jokes on stage, but that spot in the limelight has been preceded by thousands of hours of arduous work and grinding out material. It is only when speaking to Deb about the effort that goes into a routine that I begin to appreciate how much it takes to get to the point where you're ready to take to the stage.

"The social work community in Northern Ireland really got behind the idea" Deb tells me. "I emailed around my team and asked them to cascade the message on to other social workers they knew in the area to see if they'd want to come along". The response amazed

Deb and, by the time the show came around, the venue had sold out. Tentatively peering from the side of the stage to a packed-out audience, she was filled with nervous excitement about what was to come. "I still feel nervous today" Deb says when I ask about how she coped with that night. "You need to feel nervous because that's what gives you the energy to go out there and perform; that's what shows you how much it means".

The show was a success and much of the material that Deb uses in her current routine stems from that period in her life when she gave up all her free time to carry through on that random promise to her colleagues.

Coming back to Jim's first night behind the mic, he recounts a similar feeling of nervousness and the same ability to use this to fuel his performance on stage. Although his beginnings were a little humbler than Deb's and he'd been building up to his moment for longer, he tells me how making that decision to put himself up in front of an audience was nerve-wracking "no matter how many people are in the crowd".

Two social workers performing stand-up comedy in Northern Ireland who both took to the stage at around the same time, but they had no idea about each other. It sounds to me like too much of a coincidence to be more than mere fate. I've been over to Northern Ireland to train social workers and I know that the social work community is close-knit over there. There aren't many universities training students and their trust system means that there are only a handful of major employers. You can say a name of a social worker to anyone in the field and, more likely than not, they'll have heard of them before, or at least know somebody who has.

Many people in Jim's position, when on the rarely trodden path of the social work stand-up comedian, might have been slightly sceptical when finding out that somebody else had started up around the same time as he had, with a routine based on the same set of material. Instead of contacting her with claims of plagiarism, Jim reached out with an offer of friendship and sent an email to Deb to see how they might work together in future. An enduring partnership and friendship was born that day.

Now, over three years on from their decision to come together as a duo, the pair sit across from me at the dinner table and bounce off one another in a manner which suggests they've known each other all their lives. While they ended up in the same place and now spend their weekends touring their show all over the country, their backgrounds into social work were vastly different; literally at the opposite ends of the world.

Raised in foster care in her native Australia, Deb feels she has mostly fond memories of social workers through her care experience. Although some of her earliest experiences include being in and out of babies and children's homes before settling into a long-term foster family, Deb reflects how "my two main social workers stayed with me throughout my childhood. After the earlier moves and lack of a settled place to call home, I've got fond memories of that stability I found in the end. My foster parents always had time for me and let me know that I was valued, that I mattered. It's funny how you remember the little things when you look back on your childhood, like how they would stop and buy me ice-cream whenever we passed a parlour".

"It was more than just the little things though, and I will never forget how they took the time and made the effort to get to know my birth family. They knew I had divided loyalties, between the people who brought me into this world and the ones who were raising me, but they never judged me or thought any less of me for wanting to keep in touch with my birth family. I genuinely felt that my foster parents liked me as a person and it was never a burden to have me there. That means the world to somebody in foster care".

"Adolescence was difficult as I struggled to make sense of my identity, torn between my birth heritage and my upbringing in foster care. Throughout those difficulties I remember how my social worker would tell me that my past was not my responsibility and I wasn't to blame for what had come before. Instead she gave me the courage to realise that whatever I did from that day on was my choice. She promised me that she believed I could do anything I wanted with my life, and I believed her"

"That was the first time I'd ever heard somebody tell me that I could do whatever I wanted with my life or be whoever I wanted to be, that my past wasn't going to define me. Such a realisation came over me like an epiphany and I said right there and then 'I want to be like you and help other kids'. I did just that and resolved to become a social worker. When I look back on my younger years I can see how the 'can do' attitude I've still got started right then. Ever since those words from my social worker, I've always challenged myself to keep trying new things. Stand-up comedy is one of those challenges".

Jim's social work career spans three decades and has taken him from where he was raised in Northern Ireland to the North-West of England and beyond. His experiences of living and working in the, often hard and gritty, inner-cities of Manchester and Belfast come out in his routine. Starting out as a social worker during the Troubles in his homeland, Jim tells me how "social workers back then were expected to go into homes without any back-up at all, not knowing what we'd face when we knocked on a door. There was no police protection because of the threat officers would face if they went into the kind of areas we had to go into to make sure children were safe. It was frightening at times, to go alone and with nothing to protect you but your leather-backed diary, but we did it because we had to do it to protect people".

"We would have to go into the heart of South Armagh to remove children who were at risk, or do things like investigate parents' with terrorist backgrounds in their own homes. This was all done on large unpoliced housing estates without any protection at all". When I compare Jim's first forays into social work with my own, I realise just how much easier I've had it. I've been threatened, abused and intimidated more times than I can even remember, but I've always been able to call on police back up when I've needed it and have never had to face the kind of risks he's had to. No wonder he's able to take to the stage and not be intimidated by a crowd of a hundred cynical social workers.

As the time draws closer to seven o'clock, their spot on the stage looming, I ask Jim and Deb how their families cope with the fact that they give up so much of their free time to go gigging all over the United Kingdom, cheekily adding my belief that 'I can't imagine you're making a lot of money out of it all'. Jim laughs and tells me that, far from making any profit, they are grateful if they can cover the costs of the venue, hotel and travel every night; any money left over going towards the social workers Benevolent Trust that offers help to fellow professionals experiencing financial difficulties because of issues beyond their control.

"My husband and kids know that this is my thing and are happy for me" Deb says, "our aim is to put the social back into social work and to get people going out together in their team, that's why we tend to do our biggest tour around Christmas time to tie in with work parties". Hearing Deb speak of her and Jim's passion makes it clear that their only motivation to keep doing what they're doing is to entertain social workers and bring them together, the same ideal that Deb had in the team meeting three years ago when her stand up dreams began.

As we finish our meals and get ready to head back to the venue for the evening (Jim and Deb had already been there setting up before meeting me) I can't help but think of how rare people like Jim and Deb are in the world of social work. Not only is their stand-up comedy unique, but they are both veteran social workers who speak lovingly and positively about the career. Not once in our time together do I hear anything about them regretting their choice of vocation, wishing for new jobs or feeling that our profession is hopeless. I wish I could bottle up their effervescent humorous passion for social work and carry it with me.

Our venue for the evening is the back room of a pub on the banks of the river Ribble called The Continental. I take a seat near the rear of the room as Jim and Deb complete their preparations for the evening, watching as the place slowly fills up with a selection of my fellow social workers and students.

To my left is a large group of around ten social workers, all women, who are team members in one of Preston's child protection assessment teams. In high spirits (by which I mean that there is at least one bottle of wine per person on their table), they later tell me that they are here as part of their Christmas night out. Halfway through her routine, it is revealed by Deb that one of their group,

Anne, had emailed Jim and Deb to ask if there was allocated seating at the event so she could choose where to sit. This raises a great roar of laughter on the table as Deb points out that we're in the back room of a pub and it's not as if we're at a U2 concert in an arena. Deb gets a second round of laughter and Anne goes a shade redder when she adds "or maybe it was because Anne didn't want to sit next to the rest of you".

I'm joined at my table by a retired social worker who has brought her husband along for the evening and three social work students from the local University of Central Lancashire. As Deb goes around the tables as part of her warm up routine (she doubles up as opening act for Jim as well as being the main event herself) I learn that we're joined tonight by a team of adoption social workers, a group of fast-track social work trainees, more students and one of Jim and Deb's super fans who has trekked over from Hull for the evening.

In total, there are around forty people in the room by the time the lights go down and Jim turns up the volume on *Teenage Kicks* by The Undertones in the minutes before Deb takes to the stage (in the interval, Jim tells me that turning up the music to the point where people have to almost shout to be heard is an old gig trick to get people in the mood for a good night). I manage to catch a quick word with Deb before she goes on and ask her how she's feeling. "You soon get a sense of how the audience is going to be in the first few minutes, so we'll see how it goes. People have had a drink and there's a Christmas party in so it should be a good night". With that said, she sneaks away from me and to the side of the stage as Jim begins to announce her introduction over the microphone.

After her opening to the night's entertainment, Deb passes the baton over to her partner who will be providing the first half of the show. Jim begins by stating that, as a social work comedian, some of his punchlines might be late but assures everyone that he's staying up all night to complete them. If anybody doesn't get his jokes, they will be on their desk first thing the next day. It's a solid start and people are laughing with wry smiles about how many times they've made similar promises to their own managers. He moves onto a routine about his experience as a newly qualified social worker in the late eighties in Greater Manchester. Born from the true stories of life as a social worker in tough estates that he had shared with me earlier, his tales are peppered with the same dark humour that is common in offices up and down the country. He uses humour as a way of shedding light on topics many would consider off limits or taboo, but that more of us should really be open to discussing in the debate about why so many people burn out and leave our profession. He raises some big laughs, that are quickly followed by uncomfortable moans from an audience who aren't sure whether they should be laughing or not.

The latter part of his routine is centred around how to be a good social worker, harking back to the days when duffle coats, cardigans and elbow patches were what made good social workers, along with poor time keeping and disorganised filing of course. He gets a raucous reaction when he takes off his jacket to reveal a t-shirt which proudly reads, 'Even mediocre social workers make a difference', adding it provides his clients with confidence when he wears it as part of his job. He finishes off with a piece crafted from Karpman's Triangle theory on relationships that takes me back to my time learning about it as a student. He discusses with great passion how we social workers love to see ourselves as rescuers and highlights the martyrdom inherent in our professional psyche. Interspersed with jokes about how we most often rescue ourselves with wine and chocolate, he leaves on the lingering question of "who is helping the helpers?".

In the half-time interval, I catch Jim at the bar as I'm sneakily ordering a pint of shandy (I'm a Geordie, it's a Friday night and I'm in a northern city at Christmas time so trust me, I need to hide the fact that it's 9pm and I'm drinking shandy in a bustling pub). As I'd literally laughed out loud the entire routine (yes, a real life 'LOL') I tell Jim that I thought the night was going well and his material had me in stitches. "Ahh, it's going shit" he candidly tells me, looking like a little bit of the sparkle I'd seen earlier on had gone from his eyes.

Deb joins us at the bar and is of a similar mind to Jim, feeling that the audience isn't really connecting with most of their comedy tonight. "Sometimes it just doesn't work out" she tells me "and you can never really tell how it's going to shape up until you get on stage". "Everything should have been right tonight" she continues "the venue is great, there's a good number of people here, it's Christmas party time, but it's just not coming off". I try to reassure her and Jim that their material is amazing, but it gives little comfort when they both feel as if Jim's jokes are failing to connect; leaving Deb lacking in confidence that she can do any better. It reminds me of many a day I've had at work, because sometimes you can do everything right as a social worker but it just doesn't click into place.

Having had my fair share of experiences in how difficult it can be to please a social work audience with my articles and blogs (let's be honest here, we can be an awkward and finicky bunch who love to moan!) I feel for Deb as the lights go down again and she takes to the stage for her own routine. This time one of the tables is lying empty as a group of students have taken to drinking in the bar instead of watching the rest of the show.

Deb begins by reflecting that, after twenty years in the profession, she's observed that being a social worker is much like being a comedian because, "no one knows how you do it, nobody wants to do it themselves, but I guarantee they'll have an opinion or two about how you can do the job better". Deb moves on to explore the minutiae of social work office life, lamenting 'tea fund dodgers' by suggesting they are also responsible for the unwashed dishes and crummy benches, paying no heed to polite reminders wallpapered in many office kitchens due to their avoidant attachment styles. In a chat after her show, Deb makes me promise not to reveal too much of her material (after all, she'll be out on tour again this coming winter) but her set covers a wide range of topics from breastfeeding to health and safety, and nursery rhymes to Maslow's hierarchy of needs.

After Deb brings the show to an end by singing Adele's *Someone like you* (I won't spoil why she does this, but it is hilarious) the audience filters out and I'm left with Jim, Deb and their super fan from Hull. The super fan stays with us for around ten minutes as Jim and Deb thank her for the effort she's made in travelling this far. I then catch a few minutes with the super fan as she tells me what a wonderful thing the pair are doing and how she wishes there were more people out there who were trying to bring our profession together like they are. I agree that social workers need to get better at uniting and do more to support those who make great personal sacrifices to bring us together, like Jim and Deb have done this evening.

As we bid the super fan farewell and the three of us step back out into a cold, dark, wet and windy night in mid-December, Deb forlornly apologises and tells me "I wish you'd come on a better night". I can't help but feeling sad when she says that to me because, not only did I find their routine hilarious, I also appreciate the great effort they are making to give up so much of their free time in the hope that they can lift a profession that often feels so dejected, downtrodden and depressed.

We get in my car as I drive them to the station where they are due to get a train back to their hotel for the night, in nearby Manchester. During the short journey, I have enough time to share my sympathies with them about the crowd and express my wonder at how many people in social work don't 'get' the need to poke fun at what we do from time to time. "Don't worry about us, we're made of tough stuff, we're social workers" Jim tells me with a smile as I drop them off to catch the last train of the night.

Watching them walk away from me, through that cold northern rain, I can't help but marvel at just how tough and resolute they both are. You need to be resilient to be a social worker and you must have nerves of steel to be a stand-up comedian. So, this pair, giving up their free time to combine the two disciplines by becoming social work stand-ups, must be (to borrow a lyric from Bruce Springsteen) tougher than the rest.

As in life and as in our chosen career, there are good gigs and bad gigs if you're a social work stand up. Tonight was one of the less satisfying gigs for Jim and Deb, but as they turn around to give me a final wave goodbye, I doubt that this is the last I'll be seeing of them. Social workers don't give up that easy.

Chapter Two: I'm sorry I'm not the person that I used to be

I'm sorry I'm not the person that I used to be before I started this job. I know I've changed in ways that you can see and I also know I've changed in ways you can't see too. For better or worse, I recognise that I'm not the man you fell in love with, forged friendships with and watched grow up.

When I first started out in this job you know it was because I wanted to help others and make a difference in the world. I didn't want a job where I counted down the hours or counted out all the money I'd earned at the end of week; I wanted to have a working life spent in the service of others. I wanted to measure the fruits of my labour in the lives I had made better and not how much I had improved my own status.

For me, there was no finer choice of career than this. I have always been proud to be a social worker and never once regretted my decision to devote my life to it.

But I can't hide how much it has changed me as a person, for better and for worse.

I know that I'm not there for my own family as much as I used to be.

It used to be the case that I would come home at the same time every day and my word was my guarantee. If I said I would be at the school play, I would be there. If I said I would make the family meal, you could rely on me. If it was your birthday, I could always get the time off and devote all of my attention to you.

I'm sorry that it's not like that for us anymore.

You are no longer the only people that I have a duty of care and responsibility for and, as much as it pains me to say this, there are sometimes other people who need me far more than you do.

If I don't see the school play, I know our daughter will still go home safe that night. If I miss the family meal, at least I know you'll have had something to eat regardless. Even if I'm not there on your birthday, I know you'll be cared for.

It's not that I love you any less these days, just that I sometimes have to give up what makes me happy for the sake of what keeps other people safe.

I know that all of my friends have seen me slowly fade out of their lives as well.

It used to be the case that we would speak on the phone all the time but, after a day of talking so intensively to people about such terrible experiences they are enduring, it's hard to have the energy to pick up the phone one more time when I get home.

30

When you had problems, I would be your shoulder to cry on and you always used to say how great I was at offering advice. Now you think I no longer care because I don't react as passionately as I used to. It's not that I don't care, it's just that the petty arguments you have and little dramas in your life seem so trivial in the context of what I've seen in work. The little issues don't seem so important when you've spent your day working with people who have experienced abuse, oppression and injustice, the like of which you've never seen before.

It's hard to show concern about your cracked iPhone screen when I've driven a family to a food bank today and had to beg my senior managers for the money to turn their heating back on.

It's difficult to offer advice about making up with your partner after a petty falling out when I've spent the past three months seeing a mother slowly lose her children because my efforts to empower her to change her way of life have failed.

I've seen things you can't imagine and been in situations that will haunt me forever.

I know you think I'm not a good friend anymore because I don't react the same way I used to and you probably worry what you've all done wrong. But, as the clichéd old line so often used by departing lovers goes, "It's not you, it's me".

The things I've seen change you as a person and, in turn, as a friend.

I've been privileged enough to see the best and worst of human nature.

I've been abused, praised, castigated, heralded, attacked, thanked and threatened all in the same day.

The things I've seen, the burdens I bear and the duties I have to undertake don't just fade away when you get home on an evening or finish for the weekend; the emotions linger and stay with you long after the events have passed.

I can't just clock off and switch off like I used to.

But I hope all those that I love have seen me change for the better as well.

Even though I'm no longer there for you as much as I used to be, I hope you can take pride in the fact that I am there for others who don't have the same support networks that you do.

Even though I'm no longer as carefree and innocent as I once was, I hope you have seen how I've grown as a person and taken wisdom from my experiences.

Although you think my love for you has faded, I want you to know that my love has grown. Seeing how cruel humans can be to one another has made me appreciate you all the more. Seeing people find beauty in even the darkest of days has taught me that I will always stick by you because, even if times get so hard you think you can't go on, I know that I have seen people get through much worse and persevere.

I apologise to you all for not being the person that I once was and for no longer being as reliable as I used to be. I know it might sometimes look like I don't care for you as I used to, but I assure you that's not the way it is. It's just that there are sometimes people out there that need me more than you do.

I wish that wasn't the case and I wish that all the pain was gone from the world. But, until that day comes, I will continue trying to make my little corner of the world a better place. If that means having to make personal sacrifices, then that is the price that I have to pay. I'm just sorry that my choice of career burdens all of you as well.

Chapter Three: From child protection to politics

It's August 2016 when I first arrange to meet Emma Lewell-Buck and British politics is in a state of flux.

On the 23rd of June 2016, just six weeks before my initial meeting with Emma, the United Kingdom voted to leave the European Union in a landmark referendum that will change the whole landscape of the country. A fortnight after the result of the referendum was announced there is a new Prime Minister, Theresa May, in Number 10 Downing Street.

As a further knock on effect from the referendum result, Jeremy Corbyn (the leader of Emma's Labour Party) is facing a new leadership contest less than a year after sweeping to victory with a landslide vote of 59.5% at the first time of asking in September 2015. The official line from the Labour MPs contesting Corbyn's position is that he should have done far more to get Labour voters to support the remain campaign. The feeling from many others is that the majority of Labour MPs have never fully-supported Corbyn's leadership and were waiting for the first opportunity to remove him from power; the EU vote being a Trojan horse with which to do so.

When we first meet up, Emma has recently made national headlines after resigning from the post of shadow minister for devolution and local government she has held for the past seven months. She is quoted at the time as saying she felt "heartbroken at the state of the Labour Party" and was resigning in the hope that a stable opposition would be formed under a united leadership. It is a view shared by many of Emma's colleagues in Westminster and one which forms the bedrock of a leadership campaign that will see Owen Smith pitted against Jeremy Corbyn in a battle for control of the Labour Party.

Prior to the EU referendum result, there was a hope amongst many social workers in the United Kingdom that our profession was beginning to get recognition from politicians. David Cameron, the incumbent Prime Minister prior to stepping down in the aftermath of a referendum where he campaigned for the losing side, had made a high-profile speech about vulnerable children being 'let down for far too long', a new Children and Families Bill was in the consultation stage and the Government were ploughing hundreds of millions of pounds into new social work training schemes and innovative ways of working.

Some feared that this money was being spent in the wrong places and that the Prime Minister's attention was focused in the wrong places (chiefly in prioritising adoption) but many, myself included, felt that social work had been starved of attention for so long that anything bringing light to our travails was welcome.

But now, in the post-Brexit era in which I find myself meeting Emma, the world has changed and much that once was is now lost. It takes a lot for social workers and those we support to get any sort of political recognition at all, and I walk towards Emma's office feeling as if the fallout from the Brexit decision will push our profession even further down the political pecking order, as negotiations for leaving the EU will take priority over everything else debated in Parliament.

Emma's constituency, South Shields, lies on the North-East coast of England. I'm a little early for our first meeting so I take a walk along the seafront promenade and through the town's high street to get a feel for the lives of the 75,000 people she represents. It's the height of summer holiday season and the promenade is bustling with life; happy children and their parents drawn here from all over the country for a taste of traditional seaside life.

I walk up Ocean Road, famous in this region for its award-winning fish and chips from a restaurant called Colmans, and turn right onto the town's high street. The scene is far removed from what I've seen at the seaside and every other shop I walk past is either a bookmaker, takeaway or charity store. Many others are closed down and up for rent. It is a scene replicated in provincial towns all over the country as online shopping, rising costs and competition from supermarkets squeezes out all the independent shopkeepers that gave towns like South Shields such character in the past. The shops and bus stops that I walk past throng with people who look like they are of working age.

Given that South Shields has had one of the highest unemployment rates in mainland Britain for many years, it shouldn't surprise me that this is the site greeting me on my stroll through Emma's constituency. Emma herself spoke optimistically of South Shields being a "town that knows the dignity and reward that work brings" during her maiden speech to Parliament and has focused on unemployment, especially amongst young people, throughout the four years she has been a sitting MP.

When Emma raises these issues on behalf of her constituents, she speaks from the heart and from the position of having lived and breathed these problems herself; born and raised in the constituency and knowing first-hand the devastation wrought by the closure of shipyards in the eighties and coal mines in the nineties.

It is her past, the back story leading up to her remarkable rise to becoming the first female MP the area had ever seen, as well the first person born in South Shields to be elected to represent the town in Parliament, that we start talking about when we settle down to discuss Emma's journey from child protection to Parliament.

Emma's first memories of politics stem from an avid obsession with the Cold War when she was a child, sitting in front of the family television in the 1980s as Ronald Reagan and Mikhail Gorbachev began the peace processes that would eventually bring about the thawing of tensions between the superpowers a decade later. However, it was a political colossus closer to home, Margaret Thatcher, that was to shape Emma's upbringing in the most dramatic of ways and provide her with an antithesis for her own future political ideologies.

"Thatcher told everyone to buy their council houses and then closed the shipyards and mines that people were working in" she tells me when recalling the extent to which her whole upbringing was shaped by political ideology. As Emma describes this deception and subsequent abandonment of her home town by the Government of her youth, I get a sense that the impact of Thatcher's policies continues to reverberate in the constituency over thirty years later. Emma beats me to the question I am about to ask on this subject by going on to describe how "the spectre of Thatcher still looms large" over the people of South Shields she represents.

A child moulded by Thatcherism, Emma looks back and feels as if the policies that were brought in to shape her generation resulted in her and her peers being raised to "look after number one". She tells me of how "we all grew up with that sense of individualism and those messages of selfishness that were seeped into our society.

She (Thatcher) neglected her duty to look after all of her citizens by destroying the societies that were based on industries she felt were no longer of benefit to a nation she was shaping into a service economy".

The 'dignity and reward that work brings' that Emma spoke of in her first parliamentary speech is something she experienced as a child, her father being a welder in the ship yards but finding "work would dry up" through no fault of his own. Although her family always managed to "get by", with Emma's mother gaining employment as a barmaid and then a shop assistant to make ends meet, she often questioned "why is it such a fight?" for people who were desperate for work to find employment in her home town.

Alongside her childhood views of the world being forged in the decimation of traditional industries that Margaret Thatcher brought to her region, Emma looks back on the influence that her family had on her rise to where she is today. Her maternal Grandfather helped found the GMB general trade union, her paternal grandmother once staged a sit-in at Jarrow Town Hall to get a council house for her family and her father was a union member who went on strike when she was a child. Political activism and the fight for a better way of life for the working classes was in her blood.

Looking back at her heritage, Emma describes how her family were "political but not party political", always voting Labour but not actively engaging with the formal political structure in the way that she would go on to. Encouraging this silent majority to become more actively engaged in formal political processes is something that Emma sees as one of her biggest challenges. Asking her how we can go about engaging more marginalised people in politics, and addressing the antipathy that many younger people feel at this moment in time, Emma tells me "I try to do this in my own little way by using myself as an example of what can be achieved".

The first female MP the constituency has ever seen and the first politician elected to Parliament by the town that was born there, Emma's rise is certainly inspiring for people who feel as if 'safe seats' such as those in South Shields would always be given to political high-flyers and career politicians, such as the London born and Oxford educated David Miliband who held the seat before her.

"Nobody else in Parliament looks or sounds like me" Emma explains as she discusses the importance of opening the political system to people who feel disengaged and apathetic about modern statecraft. While the fact that Emma is a local woman who speaks with a broad Tyneside accent is roundly welcomed by her constituents that I will later speak to, one telling me how committed Emma is to local causes such as keeping the hospital open and bringing jobs to the region, she has faced discrimination because of this from across the parliamentary divide. "David Cameron and Nick Clegg (the Prime Minister and deputy Prime Minister at the time of her election to Parliament in 2013) were both laughing and joking to each other about my accent when I first spoke in Parliament" she tells me. Having been in the Commons Chamber myself, I know that the room is much smaller than it appears on television and imagine such mocking from the two most powerful men in the room must have been difficult for Emma to cope with.

Emma's made of stern stuff though and recounts Cameron and Clegg's snide comments about her regional dialect without batting an eyelid. Knowing at first hand the level of abuse and vitriol that social workers must face on a daily basis as part of our job, I ask Emma if her six years on the frontline of child protection helped steel her for the combative atmosphere she faces in the Commons chamber. "Social work toughened me up, gave me determination

40

and showed me I could make a change" Emma explains, before adding "I was also used to long hours too!".

Emma's journey into social work is a tale that will be familiar to many. The first in her family to go to university, Emma studied politics and media studies at her local university (Northumbria) before leaving without a clear career path ahead of her. Despite being at university during the height of 'Blairmania', she wasn't a Labour Party member during her first stint in higher education, admitting that she "didn't really see the benefit at the time". Although it's hard to imagine it now, Emma recalls how she was a "quiet student" and a "thinker" throughout her adolescence and early adulthood, preferring to sit back and listen to others before coming forth with her own views on the world. She would sometimes "day dream of being an MP" but felt that such aspirations would only ever be dreams because she used to believe that "people like me could never succeed in politics".

Looking for direction after leaving university with a thirst to make a difference in the world, Emma joined her local Labour Party but her initial impressions weren't great. She walked in to find that local party politics in her town was dominated by males and felt that her first constituency meeting was "boring". Having sat in a fair few such meetings in the past myself, I can assure you that the boredom Emma speaks of is true to form. Bouncing around a number of jobs she "didn't really like" after completing her degree, two major decisions that Emma took in 2004 were to have a dramatic effect on the rest of her life.

The first was to stand for election as a local councillor.

The second was to apply for a Masters in social work at Durham

University.

Emma's decision to become a social worker was based in the reasoned and pragmatic approach to life that I later find out is the hallmark of her success as a politician. Taking a logical look at her career options, Emma saw that there were lots of social work jobs advertised in her area. She reasoned that completing the Masters would give her a profession and she believed she could forge a successful and stable career with her skill set being suited to a caring vocation. When I ask about what her view was of social workers before she made this decision, she candidly admits that she saw us all as "detached liberal do-gooders". At least she doesn't add in the sandals and chunky woollen sweaters that have also become a stereotype of our profession.

Combining a fledgling career in local politics with full-time training to be a social worker at one of the most prestigious Universities in the country sounds like an arduous task, and Emma admits as much. I ask her what the key to managing was, given so many of us in social work struggle to get even a basic work/life balance without the additional demands of being a local councillor. "The key is to have core principles" she tells me, "to make sure that your political views match your professional views". Emma goes on to tell me that an ethical base to your decision-making is perhaps not all that is required, adding in that she worked "fifteen hours a day for seven days a week" throughout her social work education and accompanying early political career.

"There are huge similarities between politics and social work", Emma tells me, going on to share how it is these similarities that made her dual roles possible. "In its simplest form, social work is about helping individuals and politics is about helping millions, but the problems you are working to address are the same. Whether you are looking to help one constituent remain in their family home after changes to benefits have hit them with a 'bedroom tax' they can't afford, or you are looking to roll back such changes across the entire country, the issues that people face are the same".

After graduating in 2007, Emma took up her first qualified social work position within a child protection team in a Local Authority close to home. Although Emma felt like she had gone into social work with her "eyes open", having done her research into the true nature of the profession before beginning her training, the reality of being thrown into frontline child protection still came as a shock to her. The first words she uses to describe her initial steps into frontline work continue to ring true almost a decade on from when she started out: "paperwork and bureaucracy".

Feeling sucked into the paperwork and bureaucratic demands of a procedural system from day one, Emma could immediately see how a culture that prioritised paperwork over people would eventually lead to workers losing the ethos of social work and forgetting what the profession was all about. Compounded by the need for a quick turnaround of plans and high caseloads, Emma found that there was very little time for reflection and analysis on the cases she was asked to hold. In an environment that is unfortunately still familiar to many social workers that Emma engages with to this day, she found that people like herself were left to "sink or swim" in an atmosphere she describes as "quite soul-destroying".

Emma would see new workers coming into the office and baulking at what they found, telling herself "I'll give them a day before they walk out of here". More often than not she was right, with the natural effect of too many cases and not enough time leading to a high turnover in staff. This high turnover fuelled a vicious cycle where the workers who stayed, like Emma, were given more and

43

more work.

Approaching her first full year on the job, already having gained two stones in weight as a knock-on effect of the long hours and poor work/life balance, Emma was given her first Court case. At a time when most social workers should be just taking their initial steps into child protection cases, Emma was dealing with care proceedings where there were fourteen parties involved. "It really was sink or swim" she tells me, with the workers that looked like they were coping the best given more and more work as there was nobody else to take the strain. She recounts this grim time and tells me that "my manager once told me that this job would eat me up because of the kind of person I am. I was so thorough and caring that I couldn't possibly do less than my very best for people. But she was right, if you care this much and try too hard you will burn out".

Like so many people before and after her, Emma was finding that social work wasn't the job she thought it was and this left her feeling "quite disheartened" by the entire system. But what was she to do? Somebody had to do the job and, despite the battles she faced, Emma was always driven by her will to help people who had no one else fighting for them. In order to help people in the way they deserved, Emma had little choice but to endure the long hours, crippling stress and self-sacrifice needed to protect children in a toxic environment. She admits that this isn't healthy or realistic for most people, "some people have to make tough choices and can't handle the sacrifice to their families as much as others" she shares.

Fifteen-hour days, seven days a week. Given more and more demanding cases because she stuck around. Having to make tough decisions about children's whole lives with little support and hardly any time at all for reflection. Facing regular verbal abuse for simply doing her job and once grabbed by the throat in a physical assault by an irate parent. Needing a panic alarm fitted to her house, getting taken to court with police protection and held in victim support suites until it was her time to give evidence. I ask Emma how she managed to cope with all this and keep going.

"There comes a point where you just can't take it any more… you're taking it home with you every night… it feels like you're living in a parallel world filled with paedophiles and monsters and all the good is taken out of the world. I had no let up, even on holiday I would take work with me, I was unwell but I just kept thinking I could ride it out. I kept thinking it had to change for the better one day".

One day it did change, but not for the better. After fighting to keep going for so long, it all came to a head and Emma couldn't take it any longer. "I went off sick for four weeks" she candidly admits. "I was incredibly unwell". Walking out of the office in the middle of the day, taking herself to the local beach and staring out to sea, Emma realised that it had all become too much for her. Even though she went above and beyond, even though she put in all the extra hours, even though she had an innate drive to help others that she was born with, even though her managers kept showing their faith in her, social work had eventually broken her. "I swam for a while, I sank for a while, and then I swam again".

Hearing of how honestly Emma speaks about social work and how much she has experienced herself, it feels like I'm speaking to a politician who finally 'gets it'. After years of egotistical career politicians paying lip service to social workers by pretending they know the issues we face, Emma's years of actually being out there alongside her fellow social workers is a refreshing and welcome change.

After taking some time out to recover her strength and fortitude, Emma continued to rise through the ranks of local politics and was the lead member for adult services in South Tyneside by the time David Miliband announced he would be standing down as an MP, triggering a local by-election. When the opportunity came up to apply to be Labour's candidate, Emma sought the advice of her uncle who was terminally ill at the time. One day when she was sat by his bedside in the local hospital she asked him if she should try for selection, fearing that the safe seat would be bestowed upon a rising star or one of the party's "chosen ones". He told Emma "look pet, you've worked towards this your whole life, do it, try".

Putting in her application form on a Friday afternoon, she was called later that same night and asked to be in London the next day for an interview. Quizzed by a panel including the Labour Party grandees Keith Vaz and Angela Eagle, Emma travelled home in tears on the train fearing she'd blown her chance. She didn't have the time to make the political connections others had established and she couldn't have afforded the specialist political interview training others were able to fund; fearing that this left her out of her depth. A sixty-hour working week in social work, local council role and fitting in time with her family meant that she felt somebody more suited to career politics would get the shot at representing her own community over her.

While still in tears from the feeling she hadn't made the cut, she received a phone call on the train back North telling her she was going through to the next stage, an internal election by her local party members to select their chosen candidate. With four weeks of canvassing ahead of her, Emma went into work on Monday morning to ask her manager for the leeway in her workload that would give her the shot at her dreams she had always longed for. Her request for four weeks of unpaid leave was dismissed out of hand, resulting in Emma spending all day campaigning and then coming home to complete assessments and reports every night. Even when being handed an opportunity such as this, Emma found that her personal needs came a very distant second to her employers need to meet timescales.

Towards the end of her campaign, as the groundswell of support from within the town she had always called home made it increasingly likely that she was going to be selected as the local candidate, Emma went to see her manager and asked if she could do a final visit to say goodbye to the children she had given so much of her life to. This request was denied by her manager who callously told her "they'll know what's happened when they see you on television". Four years on from her election victory, Emma shares how "to this day on, it still breaks my heart that I never got to say a final goodbye to the children".

With a career that she had given so much for and a rise to Parliament that could inspire many local young women to aspire to more in their lives, it is lamentable that Emma never had a proper last day as a social worker, or even the simple opportunity to say goodbye to the people she tried so hard for every day. As with so much of what she tells me during our meetings, I see her own tale mirrored in the lives of many other social workers across the world. As soon as we are seen as expendable or on our way to a new position, we are often ushered out of the door with as little fuss and ceremony as possible.

In under two months, Emma had gone from a practising social worker to being an elected Member of Parliament; thrust into the national spotlight as the replacement for a man that many had tipped to be a future Prime Minister. In March, she was sat in an office typing up assessments and case notes, in May she was sat across from David Cameron in the Palace of Westminster. Intrigued by the practicalities of how someone copes with such a sudden change, I ask Emma about the day-to-day responsibilities that come with becoming a member of Parliament for the first time.

The good news is that the long hours, analytical skills and ability to handle stress that came from her six years in social work gave Emma the prowess to hit the ground running in the cut and thrust world of politics. Returning to the jibes made about her accent by David Cameron and Nick Clegg during her first speech in Parliament, such remarks pale into insignificance compared to the daily abuse she had to face as a social worker. The bad news is that, however prepared she felt she was to distinguish herself as a politician and serve her constituents to the best of her ability, Emma found the practicalities of becoming an MP difficult to cope with at first.

"The first day I walked into Parliament, it hit me how I was going to be alone. I had become a small businesswoman overnight and there was constant pressure to get everything set up in the first few months. I had to find my own office and staff members. In social work, I had been trained for the job I was going into and I knew my responsibilities, but there's nothing that can prepare you for your first days as an MP". It's those little things about the day-to-day reality of being a politician, setting up an office and hiring your own staff, that are lost to so many people looking in at politics from the outside. Even as somebody who has a fair level of interest in politics, I had no idea that Emma was basically left to her own devices in setting up her own office and employing the staff that came with it.

Comparing the stress and strains that came with her child protection role to her first steps into national politics, Emma laughs and tells me how much easier it is for her to handle being a Member of Parliament. The most obvious sign of the difference between the role she had left and the one she was commencing came when her mother told her "it's like the colour has come back into you" after she found out she'd won the by-election and was bound for London. The years of stressful working conditions, sixty hour weeks and often unbearable pressure had taken their toll on her.

Despite the struggles she faced throughout her time as a social worker, Emma continues to miss the profession. In one of our interviews she tells me "what I miss most is the direct relationship with people and changing lives with a one-to-one connection". It is this desire to connect with people and help others that means Emma looks forward to her fortnightly surgeries with her local constituents more than any other aspect of her job, although the recent death of her fellow MP Jo Cox has meant her staff have had to review Emma's security measures considering Jo's horrific murder at the hands of one of her own constituents.

Re-elected in 2015 with 51% of the vote (albeit with a reduced majority due to a UKIP that was increasingly making inroads into Labour's heartlands at the time) and made Shadow Minister for Children and Families not long after our last interview, Emma has come a long way from the day she sat staring out to sea and coming to terms with the realisation that social work had burned her out. She has come an even longer way from the little girl who took an interest in politics during the eighties but feared she would never make it because nobody in Parliament looked or sounded like her.

Her personal ambition to become a politician realised and four years on from when she last worked as a social worker, I ask Emma how she thinks things have changed since she started out a decade ago. It would be nice to have an optimistic message about improvement but Emma doesn't want to lie to me (dispelling another stereotype I've held about politicians for a long time) and gives me her honest opinion that "things have got worse. The Government shackles social workers with bureaucracy, paperwork and mistrust that permeates throughout every process of the profession. Successive governments feel legislation is needed as a response to every high-profile child death. When did we became such an untrusting society?".

Emma also feels that the poor public image of social work is having a devastating effect on the morale of workers and creating barriers to effective work with people who have been conditioned by the media to believe social workers are incompetent. "People don't see the excellent work that social workers do every day, they only hear about social work if things go wrong" she passionately explains. "We're the same as the police, you only hear bad news about us. You can make massive physical and emotional changes to the lives of those in need, but none of that is ever picked up on in the media. If people could only see the outcome of our work, the complete difference that comes over children when they're properly cared for, we'd have a much better public image". The fact that Emma uses the term 'we' shows me that, even if she is no longer professionally registered, in her heart she still sees herself standing alongside the rest of us as a social worker.

As with much of what Emma tells me in person, or I latterly read of as I continue to follow her work in the local and national press, her words chime well with those of us still out there trying our hardest to make a difference in the world of social work. There is a feeling that the profession finally has a politician who understands the issues we face at first hand and has practised in recent memory. Without wanting to place too much pressure on her, I put it to Emma that it's all well and good talking about the issues we face, but what does she hope to do about tackling them and moving beyond the professional echo chamber?

For a start, she sets out her belief that one of the key issues we currently face is that our profession has never had a minister or Secretary of State who truly understands the reality of frontline social work practice. I feel Emma speaks on behalf of most of the country when she expresses her belief that people occupying positions with departmental responsibilities have a moral obligation to immerse themselves in the role. Alas, we both share the belief that most politicians either don't make the effort to learn what it's like to work in the jobs their departments arc responsible for, or have an ideologically driven agenda of what those jobs should be. Making sure we get someone in position who truly understands social work, or helping the current incumbents to see the profession beyond what they are presented with by civil servants and senior managers, would be a fine start she tells me.

The next issue we face is one of getting our case heard by the powers that be. As it stands, in this profession we are all too familiar with the way in which our work only attracts attention when there are failings. When these high-profile failures do come along, most often when children are killed by their own parents, the same old line is trotted out that 'lessons will be learned' and we enter a process of drafting new legislation that aims to regulate away the fact that some parents are driven to harm their own children. As it currently stands, Emma believes that there are two monolithic barriers that occupy the thinking of politicians at the expense of all other public sectors: health and education services.

"Adult social care is clumped in with health and children's social care is clumped in with education" she tells me before going into further detail about the impact this has for people like her who are striving to put social work on the political agenda. Being joined to other areas of public service that dwarf our own in terms of staff and resources (there are almost 500,000 teachers in the UK and 1.2 million people working for the NHS, compared to 90,000 social workers) means that we are often pushed to the back of the queue when it comes to getting our voices heard. This doesn't put Emma off and she explains how she tries to "fit a social work question in" wherever she can, something that has been made easier with her two separate roles in the Shadow Cabinet.

Of course, Emma's ability to bring about meaningful change is hampered by the fact that the Labour Party remains in opposition, albeit in the ascendency. I'd love for us to be in government" she tells me, speaking the obvious truth that a party in perpetual opposition will fail to bring about the changes she dreams of. Asking her about the changes she would wish to see, Emma raises her fear that there is a "privatisation agenda" that aims to eventually see social work taken over by business interests. She thinks that this way of thinking, believing that all our problems are financial and can therefore be solved by ridding the burden of supporting vulnerable people from the public purse, is folly.

Instead of this covert drive towards privatisation as the panacea for all our problems, Emma believes there needs to be a root and branch overhaul of the systems that social workers use every single day. She hints at having a "secret blueprint" for revolutionising social work that she's been working on and, while she won't give me any specific details, she does set out the following issues as being critical if those in power are serious about improving social work:

- Local Authorities need to be bought out of long-term contracts with IT providers who are not fit for purpose. In place of ineffective recording software, a national system should be implemented that allows social workers to use simple but effective case management systems.

- Social work processes need to be streamlined by taking on board much of what Eileen Munro proposed in her review seven years ago (Munro, 2011).

- Employers need to have more faith in their practitioners and step back from constantly focussing on a risk-aversion model.

- The Government must stop their "obsession with adoption" and look at more effective early intervention to prevent children needing to come into the care system in the first place.

- We must move away from "big showy announcements" from the Government about social work changes and go back to basics by ensuring we can do the job we are there for; supporting current workers as well as attracting new ones to fill the gaps left by all those burning out and walking away forever.

- The hidden privatisation agenda, where there is a supposed secret will for services to fail so they can be opened to business saviours, must be reversed. We've already seen that opening health services, prisons and adult social care up to non-governmental business interests hasn't worked so we don't want this to happen to statutory social work.

In a post-Brexit world of alternative facts, Donald Trump's divided America, a supposed ten more years of austerity and political lurches to the right all over Europe, many people would say that Emma's blueprint for saving social work will never see the light of day. But, after spending a fair bit of time getting to know her and following Emma closely in the news, I'm not so sure about that. The first in her family to go to university, the first female MP her constituency has ever seen, the first politician in a long time that social workers can relate to and now back on the opposition front benches for a second time, Emma is a perfect example of the "dignity and reward that work brings" which she spoke of in her maiden speech.

With a Labour Party on the rise again following the snap election in June 2017, we might be seeing Emma on the front benches of the Government sooner than I thought when I met her for the first time the summer before. Her blueprint will hopefully be ready to reveal in all its glory by the time she makes it there.

Chapter Four: Our adult social care system is in crisis

Our adult social care system is in crisis and the impact it is having on our hospitals is disastrous.

I am a frontline service manager of a hospital social work team and in eight years of working in this area I have never seen it so bad.

My team are the social workers who meet families at their lowest, when their loved ones are in their dying days and all hope is lost. We are there at times when people are coming to terms with the grim reality that life is drawing to a close for them or their dear family members. Our social workers are there to support people who are facing illness, the rapid onset of death and the loss of all the things that made them who they once were.

My staff are also the ones who are tasked with assessing support levels and what care a person needs to help them ideally return home, or move into care placements. These placements can barely break even because the local councils pay less than half of what it costs to care for people. This sees costs being passed back to the individual, despite all the tax they have paid down the years, or their families. Homes are often put up for sale shortly after we find these placements.

My staff are the ones who assess a person's mental capacity to make decisions about all manner of things to do with their life. They are the ones who investigate safeguarding issues when abuse happens and our clients come through our hospital's accident and emergency department because of it.

My staff are the ones who get pushed to their limits, who are expected to complete extensively detailed assessments within the same day they come in so that the client can hopefully leave hospital sometime this month (because same day discharge is near impossible).

My staff are the ones who get repeatedly spoken to by fellow professionals like they are the lowest of the low because we bear the brunt of everyone's frustration at the total lack of community services that lead to acute beds being blocked. I hate the term 'bed blockers'. These aren't 'bed blockers', they are people with nowhere else safe to go to.

These acute beds being 'blocked' are fewer than ever, in hospitals that are more grossly understaffed than ever before.

Acute beds that hold the most complex and frail comorbidities in patients' health issues because modern medicine keeps people living longer and longer.

And yet my staff are the ones who keep coming in, working all the hours God sends, and somehow finding a positivity to keep calm and carry on amid of this chaos.

I often worry that we are getting close to all these wonderful people, who have chosen to give their working lives to social work, breaking down and leaving not only their jobs with us in the hospital, but the profession entirely.

The sad truth is that all of us in health and social care are being slowly but surely broken.

This truth is mirrored in the cold hard reality that the NHS itself is slowly dying and, having pushed it to the edge of the precipice, the Government appears to now be sealing the deal by failing to adequately invest in social care. This chronic underfunding means that the pressure and pace in hospital social work teams is at such an intense level that patients are undoubtedly placed at risk of harm because decisions are rushed and mistakes are made by staff who are extremely stressed.

I am scared for my future. I am scared for the future of all my colleagues across health and social care. I am scared for the future of all the patients we work with.

We don't need plans from NHS England, we need them to listen to those at the frontline who are living, breathing and crying because of this every day. We need action and we need funds to support this, not cuts. We can't bear the brunt of any more cuts without going under for good.

'Winter Pressures' are no longer an issue because the crisis is now all year round.

If we are to keep people safe at all, something must change.

Care staff are paid close to minimum wage on a zero hours basis. Agencies and homes can't afford to pay them more because Councils pay them so little, but then the agencies can't recruit so rotas can't be covered and people can't go home from hospital because there is no care waiting for them.

It's all very simple and it doesn't take an executive on half a million pounds a year to come up with a solution to this crisis. Invest more money in the sector, respect the workers for what they are doing and let us do our job in a way that not only protects people, but supports their choice and basic rights to live in a way they wish.

When asked by friends to tell them what it's like to work this way, I have often struggled to find words to explain how it feels to be in hospitals that are so utterly broken, but enraged, devastated and beyond angry are a start.

People need to realise just how bad it is, and the message needs to be understood that our NHS and entire adult social care system is falling apart. This crisis has been years in the making and only emergency surgery can save it now.

Chapter Five: And it wears you out, it wears you out

Many exceptional stories begin with a tragedy and my journey into social work started with the death of my first true love. I was 28 years old when he left this world and, when I look back, it feels like he really was the love of my life. I've gone on to marry, have children, forge a successful career and have experienced all the highs and lows that a richly lived life entails, but nothing really compares to those first promulgations of promises of eternal passion. Love, like everything else in this world, gets less special the more you grow accustomed to it. Nobody could ever match up to that first romantic love, and his loss left me rudderless and bereft.

Faced with the prospect of going on trying to live the same life that we'd once shared, or attempting to forge a new one in a place where everything didn't remind me of the love I'd lost, like a considerable number of people before me I packed my bags and headed for the bright lights of London to start over. I drifted around various retail positions and, over time, began to find joy in my life again. My laughs became less hollow, my smiles became more genuine and colour started to seep back into my world.

As I found my verve and spirit coming back, I began to think about my own needs once more, no longer feeling selfish for daring to put myself first, as if it was an affront to the memory of my lost love. When my partner was ill, I had taken a keen interest in nursing and was enraptured seeing the selfless way they worked so hard to alleviate the pain of others. Seeing their commitment brought back memories of volunteering I'd done as a young girl, helping at a children's home not far from where I lived on the North-East coast of England. I fancied nursing, but I also thought about other caring professions too.

A friend of mine who worked for one of the many borough councils in London heard about my ambitions to work with people and, a little naughtily, slipped me a jobs list that was only supposed to be seen by internal candidates. Trying my luck and applying for one of these open positions, I found myself employed in a residential children's home thanks to my voluntary experience many years prior. That was where my social work journey began.

Local Authorities were quick to spot talent and committed to nurturing their own staff in those days (which seems so far removed from the modern environment of having to offer massive relocation packages and rely on agency staff to fill teams) and, when my passion for the young people we were supporting started to show, I was seconded to a local university to gain my social work qualification. Looking back, it felt as if we were all learning how to be social workers on the job and the time spent in the classroom simply added to the skills that we were already practising with real people on a daily basis.

Being able to select future social workers from your own workforce meant that councils could see the quality and commitment of people before investing in their long-term training. It was good for the workers too because, having had the chance to work with the same people we would go on to support as social workers, we could see if the job was right for us or not. Some of the best social workers I've ever known have come through the secondment system. Those days seem so far removed from the current way of recruiting social workers that sees councils investing in their workforce based on short interviews that reward the most academic and smoothest talking of candidates. Added to that, there are so many students out there these days who have been unable to get a statutory placement through their university and are left woefully underexperienced for work through no fault of their own.

It's terribly ironic that, at a time when I was so heavily invested in campaigning for a brighter future with the miners strikes and Campaign for Nuclear Disarmament, those days were to be the highpoint of a profession that I have dedicated so much of my life to. Life is just a series of peaks and troughs. You don't know whether you're in a trough until you're climbing out, or on a peak until you're coming down. Little did any of us know that the eighties were to be a peak for social work and we'd be coming down ever since.

Those halcyon days of my early forays into the profession were a high because social workers seemed to be far more respected back then. There wasn't this public image that social workers were incompetent and there were far fewer negative stories about the profession in the media. Part of this shift may be that thresholds have changed over the years and we are perhaps spreading ourselves too thinly these days, but I believe that most of it was down to the fact that social workers offered a far better service to people when I started out. Because we spent more time with families and offered more help, we were naturally more respected for our roles due to people being able to see a tangible outcome from our work. Compare that to a modern system of risk-aversion, complex paperwork trails and social workers spending limited time with families, and it's easy to see why our public image has since soured.

After gaining my social work qualification, I was allowed the time and space to develop as a practitioner and flourished for being given the chance to grow in a nurturing environment. To borrow a phrase from the old workshop apprentice days of my parents' era, I 'served my time' and learned how to be a social worker from the ground up. There wasn't this modern culture where people are pushed far too quickly into social work through fast-track training schemes and management development programmes. Instead, we were given time. Time to develop at our own pace. Time to do our work. Time with the people we were there to support.

People would be shocked if they knew just how little time some of the most senior figures in modern social work, very well-known people whom I've managed, spent practising as frontline social workers before moving onto supposedly better things. Not in those days when I was starting out though. In those days, you were given time to shine. With smaller caseloads, team clerks and effective admin support in place, social workers were free to do the jobs that we were there to do and truly help people make a difference in their lives. We've moved so far from those nurturing working environments that it's scary to look back and see just how much we took for granted.

But we did take it for granted and then, slowly but surely, everything began to change for the worse.

One of the first shifts came about in 1988 when children's homes began to close *en masse.* We were all told that children were better off in foster homes in order that they could experience what was deemed a more 'normal' way of life. There was little recognition that some young people being moved out of residential homes wouldn't suit fostering because traditional family life doesn't work for everyone. Many of the young people we were moving had experienced the most awful abuse and neglect when living in family units and had learned to thrive in alternative environments. But, even though the fifties ideal of the nuclear family was rapidly fading out as a societal norm, we closed children's homes and moved their residents into foster care as a blanket policy. It didn't work out as well as it looked like it would on paper.

The next set of changes came in as a knock-on effect of the recession that began in the Autumn of 1990. It was around then that the terms 'streamlining', 'specialisation' and 'modernisation' first began to rear their ugly heads in social work. Although we heard those words, the difference between that recession and the more recent global recession that hit in 2008 was that the directors and senior management did far more to absorb pressures back then. That's what good managers should do, absorb the pressure from above as best they can and keep social workers protected from issues that are outside of their control. Although, as I was later to learn, holding onto that pressure for so long comes at a cost.

Back then our directors did a fantastic job of balancing the books in a way that still allowed us to operate effectively in a calm and positive environment. There wasn't the constant fear of cuts, consultations and transformation programmes that seem to hang over workforces for years in the modern world of social work. Instead of passing the pressure down and looking to ease the burden on themselves by doing so, the directors where I first plied my trade took it on their shoulders to do everything in their power to protect their workforce. Noble people from an era where there was immense pride in accepting responsibility instead of shirking it.

After the best part of a decade as a social worker, I knew I was ready to make the step up and so I became a practice manager in 1995. I loved the job, I loved the social workers I managed and I loved the work we did. Sadly, that honeymoon period didn't last forever and, around a year or so into my management career, the tide that our directors had so valiantly held back began to swell over their defences and flood into all aspects of social work practice. By 1996 we were facing bigger caseloads, increasing numbers of complex issues and more referrals coming in than ever before. Compounding these heightened pressures were the budget cuts from the last recession that started to bite, a lack of replacements for staff going on maternity or long-term sick leave, and a sharper inspection regime.

1996 was the year when the issues that beset modern social work began to clearly show themselves for the first time. It was also the year that the fabled 'restructures' began to take placc in my borough of London. From 1996 to when I left that council eight years later, I went through three different periods of restructuring. If that sounds bad, which it is, then save some of your sorrow for social workers in other areas who faced restructures even more often than we did. A restructure every two and a half years was not unusual in the slightest, it was the norm across the country. Some places were going through upheavals every year.

Out of all three restructures, the only move that made any sense was to centralise our services so that we were all based in the same building. This cut down travel times, shortened meetings and greatly improved communication between teams. It was also one of those rare changes that benefited both social workers and the people we support, as well as saving money. Every other change borne out of restructuring was driven by financial motivations and top-down guidance from people far removed from the lives of social workers and, most importantly, the reality of those that we went to work to support.

Even before these changes came into play and made life more difficult for us, the looming spectre of the dreaded 'restructure' created a dark cloud over every aspect of our work as we feared what changes were to come a long time before they did. It was all handled very badly and negative rumours about who might be losing their jobs and which departments were to be downsized were allowed to run rife for months on end. It was like one of Franz Kafka's parables, only we were living in his nightmarish vision of a dystopian authoritarian future every single day.

By the end of the third restructure, I'd had enough and it was time for me to leave after almost two decades of service to the same council. Although I say the same council, it was all but unrecognisable from the one who had taken me in with open arms and so tenderly raised me as a social worker in the eighties. Not only was the council drastically different, but my profession was too.

The constant shifting of our professional goalposts saw more children's services departments doing poorly in inspections as they struggled with adjusting to the latest ways of working. Never one to shirk a challenge though, my next move saw me joining an authority in special measures to manage a child protection team. As is so often the case, a damning inspection report gave the opportunity to start afresh and we embraced this new-found freedom to focus on recruiting a new wave of impassioned social workers. A global recruitment drive saw my team filled with people from all over the world. From North America, to Europe and on to Africa, we had an eclectic and diverse team who brought worldwide skills and training with them. With supportive management and creative ways of working that focused on the needs of the people we were there to help, not the needs of the system, we created a high-functioning workforce that soon saw us taken out of special measures.

If these positive changes had been brought about ten years previously, I would have likely been left where I was and given the time to allow my team to continue flourishing. Instead, in an era where change was becoming the norm and you had to learn to thrive in chaos, the effective operation of my team came to the notice of those above me and I was headhunted for a head of service position. Onwards and upwards I went.

For all the changes that I'd gone through up until then- restructures, inspections, new computer systems and drastic cuts to support services to name but a few- I'd never really felt scared in the workplace until that next step up to be a head of service. Yes, the process of repeated restructuring was difficult and having to turn around a failing department was hard work, but I'd never felt fearful about getting up and going to the office in the morning. I'd learned that I couldn't change the sea of unwanted progress in social work, but I could shift my sails to carry my team and the people on their caseloads along with the waves. I tried to carry that ethos of caring with me into my next step up the managerial chain of command, but the resistance to that way of working is what brought the fear.

As bizarre as this sounds, I started getting picked on for daring to look after the social workers who were out there helping families and working so hard. I'd always believed that it was the job of senior management to protect staff, look after them and give them the confidence to go out there and do the job that they knew best. I did not believe it was my job to micro-manage social workers or bend people to my will through fear and intimidation. Although this outlook on management being supportive seemed obvious to me, with it having been modelled to remarkable success by those above me when I first started out as a social worker, I found this ethos out of place in the upper echelons I was now operating within. Instead of the caring environment I'd hoped for, I found myself working within a macho culture where bullying was allowed to run rampant. Rather than focussing on supporting social workers who were struggling, the topic of conversation in meetings would routinely turn to how we could 'get rid' of staff who were seen to be underperforming.

When it became clear that I was marked as the odd one out for daring to care for social workers, I handed in my notice and went back to the area where I'd first started out. But by that time, it was too late and the rot had set in everywhere. The malaise of modernity I hoped had only infiltrated one borough was spreading across the profession that I had given so much of my life to. Taking a step back into my old stomping ground gave me a few added years of respite from the macho bullying culture I'd experienced across the border, but it didn't hold back the river forever. The profession that I loved so dearly was permanently changing.

As I look back on my days as a head of service in both of those councils, I still can't see myself acting any differently, even with the hindsight of knowing the personal cost I later paid for my efforts. I treated all my social workers as whole people, took an interest in their personal lives and empathised with the struggles they were facing. I'd done their job for almost a decade myself, so how could I not know what they were going through and appreciate their efforts? I respected my social workers, I cared for them, I supported them and I trusted them to do the jobs that they were trained to do, without resorting to micro-management or bullying.

I'm not saying that my fellow senior managers didn't care as much as me, more that their focus and personal resources were spent elsewhere. Whereas most other managers looked up to please the people above them, one day hoping to fill that position themselves, I looked down to make sure that the social workers who were doing the ground work were cared for. Because my focus was going in the direction of where the work was being done, I never remember feeling like I didn't have the time to care for people. It didn't take much effort to ask someone how they were coping or to take an interest in people's personal lives. Social workers were more than just cogs in a machine, they were people too.

Like most of us in this profession, I'm not too good at self-pro-motion and it can make me feel a little awkward to look back and praise myself for all the good I achieved. When I was a social worker I always let the families I was supporting take the credit for the positive outcomes and, when I was managing social workers, I always let them take the credit for the outcomes they helped other people achieve. I've always seen the social work role as one of facilitating and empowering, not one of doing on behalf of others. However, if I dare allow myself a rare moment of hubris, I have an excellent record of achievement throughout my years of service. I've built a solid reputation, achieved many great outcomes for children, earned the respect of my staff and developed a great deal of novice practitioners into capable and conscientious social workers.

I know managers get a tough time from social workers, but I have really loved the people I have supervised down the years. I am so proud of what I have seen people achieve, often working against the odds and in hazardous conditions to bring about positive change for vulnerable children. I have seen such brave, talented, devoted and selfless people in this line of work and I am truly grateful to have known them.

But they were more than just colleagues and this is more than a job. It's never 'just' work when you're a social worker, it's your life.

Those that I spent the best years of my life alongside never had to knock on my door because it was always open to them. They could phone me at 10.30pm any night they were worried about a court case the next day, or had dealt with an emergency placement, because they knew I always had a plan. I was wholly accountable and always on hand to back up my workers because we were in it together.

If something went wrong and there was a problem, it was our problem. If there was a setback on one case, we all pulled together to make things right. When the successful outcomes came around, we all celebrated. But, if it was my decision and my decision alone, I carried the can and shouldered the burden of blame. I believe I did everything I could to keep both the children we cared for and the workers I supervised as safe as they could be.

Then it all went wrong.

It was early 2013 when I began to realise that I wasn't the same person I used to be. I started feeling tired all the time and began to sense anxiety in run of the mill challenges I once took breezily in my stride. I used to think that burnout hits people like a speeding freight train in the middle of the night, suddenly, sharply and without warning. Or maybe it was like the straw breaking a camel's back, with everything going okay until you snap with the weight of one too many burdens to carry. That wasn't my experience at all. Crippling anxiety came upon me like a slow-moving tide, creeping in inch by inch with me barely noticing the encroaching waves. With my focus on the horizon we were all trying so hard to reach, I was knee-deep in quicksand and at risk of being lost to the murky waters before I even knew what was happening.

Because my gaze was always looking towards the goals on the horizon, of making it through the next inspection, cutting our re-referral rates, improving outcomes for children and building settled teams, I nonchalantly dismissed those first signs of my body trying to tell me that all was not right in the world I had built for myself. I put the tiredness down to my advancing years and blamed my new-found anxiousness on a 'challenging environment'. Able to pin the blame for these symptoms on my own physical health and a working culture that had become the norm in child protection, I soldiered on and tried my best to bury my fears deep inside. It worked for a while and I managed to keep my internal voice, that was screaming out to tell me something was wrong, drowned out with the hubbub of constant work.

You can't keep that up forever though, no matter how hard you try and how many times you keep beating yourself up for not being strong enough to cope. Things fell apart when I had some issues in my personal life and there was no acceptance about these at all from my managers. Instead of support, I was faced with repeatedly being told to 'man up' by men who were above me in the Council hierarchy. That was when it dawned on me just how poorly I was thought of as a person and how little acknowledgment there was for my life outside of work. Looking back, I can't remember even one time where somebody asked me how my family were doing during that difficult period in our lives. Instead of caring words of support and empathy, I was being told to 'man up' and get on with the job. I shamefully bowed to these sexist bullying comments and, once again, tried to quell my fears.

This time was different though. This time the inner-voice screaming at me to take a step back from it all, lest I send myself to an early grave, would not be muffled out. Instead of using every ounce of energy to drown out the voice by throwing myself deeper and deeper into the challenges I faced at work, I instead learned to live with the voice and crippling anxiety became part of my everyday life.

70

Anxiety harms people in many ways and, for me, one of the main symptoms was a constantly churning stomach that left me hardly able to eat at all. Breakfast passed me by daily and I would leave home with an empty stomach every morning. With a malnourished and run-down body, constantly depleted by the demands of an anxiety-fuelled limbic system, it was little wonder that I caught pneumonia by the time winter came around. Winter 2013 had some bitterly cold days but, with the order to 'man up' ringing in my ears and the fear that taking extended sick leave would mean letting down everyone who was relying on me at work, I kept getting up every morning and dragging myself into the office. I'd then drag myself back home again at the end of the day and isolate myself in my bedroom; trying to lose myself in the pages of a book.

Having worked with so many people who'd experienced it themselves, I knew the signs of depression long before I was diagnosed. By the time my family forced me to go along to talk about my problems with a doctor, it was a forgone conclusion that he was going to tell me I was depressed. The only surprise was that I'd lasted so long without needing an intervention of my own; I'd been focused on the lives and needs of others instead.

I was prescribed sleeping tablets which, looking back, was the worst thing my doctor could have done for me because I quickly became dependent. Instead of dragging myself to the office, losing myself in work and then coming home in the hope of falling asleep, I was dragging myself to the office, losing myself in work and then coming home to pop a sleeping tablet. The only thing I ever looked forward to was the sweet release of sleep that those little tablets offered me.

My family, as supportive as anyone could have hoped for, tried in vain to make me take a break from work, but I failed to heed their warnings. Instead of lancing the boil by leaving my job, I kept going. My new survival tactic was one of going through the motions in a robotic manner, keeping my mind busy at all times to distract it from the reality that the workplace environment was crushing my soul. Another short-term survival tactic that, for a time, kept me going. The results were good, my team was happy and I did everything expected of me in the workplace. I had become the martyr I'd always promised myself I never would.

In the past, the cost of my short-term coping mechanisms had been my physical and then my mental health, but those resources had been withered to shreds by now. This time the price I paid was my peace of mind, existing in a constant state of 'fight or flight' to keep up the calm exterior as I went about my work. When things got on top of me I would calmly go to the bathroom, lock myself in a toilet cubicle, cry until my tears ran dry, re-do my makeup and wander back into the office as if nothing had happened. There was no space for weakness in senior management.

I'm convinced that there must be at least one person like me in every social work department all over the world, somebody who only feels like they can function in the eye of the storm and whose life is totally shut down outside of work. Somebody in every social work department with crippling anxiety that prevents them from sleeping, eating, socialising with friends and being emotionally connected to their family every single day.

Carrying the pain and trauma for up to seven hundred children at a time, making those big decisions about whether young people should return to their birth parents or not, reading the harrowing accounts of damaged little lives and feeling the pain of parents who could not safely care for their young ones because of the damage they had suffered themselves. Then having to cope with all that at the same time as feeling victimised because you had the audacity to care about your social workers as if they were human beings. How could all those years of coping with all those things not have taken such a toll on me?

Every action was driven by fear and the constant threat of inspection. Every decision was framed within the question 'what would Ofsted say?'. And all this set against a backdrop of devastating cuts to services and a failure by successive governments to address the sorry state of our profession.

For all the pressure, I kept my anxiety hidden and pushed on through for far longer than I had any right to. I had many social workers and hundreds of children who were reliant upon me and I couldn't let them down. I was the coper. I was the one who dealt with the problems. I was the one who carried the can. That was who I was.

I kept it all locked deep inside me for three years and learned to live in constant fear. I didn't want to be seen as weak or unreliable. I didn't want people to lose their faith in me and God forbid I would dare take any sickness leave, there was no time for that. I couldn't keep running from the monster forever though and, earlier this year, in a job which I still had a lot of love in my heart for, it caught up with me. The dizzy spells increased, I became more exhausted than ever before and my stomach cramps intensified.

I felt spaced out and detached. I was scared all the time. I would hide in the office toilets and cry more often than ever. Three times I collapsed on the commute home.

I knew something was wrong but I was trying so desperately to hold on, to be there for the job I had given my working life to and for all the people who relied on me. Eventually, in desperation, my husband bypassed our doctor and took me straight to our local hospital where I collapsed on the floor and was carted off for tests as soon as I made it through the doors.

They diagnosed me with complete mental and physical exhaustion, depression, panic disorder and PTSD. I told the Consultant what I did for a living and she wasn't even surprised at how I'd ended up this way.

For a while, life was a blur and it was impossible to work. I couldn't even walk, I was heavily medicated and I had to be looked after like a baby. Despite all that I was coping with, do you know what the worst part was? The worst part was that I hated myself for being weak.

I felt so weak that I wanted to die because I believed I was no use anymore. Never mind that I had the most wonderful husband and children who, incidentally, all begged me never to return to the job I loved, I felt useless all the same. I thought I should kill myself and one dreadful day I attempted to do it. My professional and personal lives were indistinguishable and I believed I could no longer be myself if I could no longer do my job.

Somehow, I pulled myself back from the edge and, as I share my story with you, I'm now on the road to recovery. With fantastic support from mental health services and my family, a long journey of self-discovery has begun. Now the challenge is to find out who I am if I can no longer be the rock who supports everyone else. In social work, there is a culture where we are expected to simply absorb all the pain, pressure and panic that comes our way. Those who look like they're invulnerable to burnout are heralded and, for

74

a long time, I took pride in being invincible myself.

That gift of invincibility came at a great price for me and, to keep the lie going that I was coping, I had to quell the little voice inside that always asked 'if you're looking after everybody else, why can't you look after yourself?'. I tried shutting that voice out by burying it, distracting it, drowning it out with work and medicating it to the point I numbed all my feelings. What I learned in the end was that little voice was the very thing that made me who I was as a person. It was my childhood memories, my teenage dreams and my adult personality. That voice was what made my heart thump, what brought colour to my world and what gave me the power to love. It was my soul.

I'm here on the other side and I'm getting better all the time, but I know that others haven't been as lucky as me and I realise that there are many more people out there who are still going through what I was. It would be easy for me to tell those of you reading my words to simply get up and walk out of your jobs if you feel the same way as I used to. Easy to say, but not easy to do.

I was close to retirement by the time it became all too much for me to bear any longer, my age and financial position affording me a certain sense of freedom not enjoyed by most. People must work to survive and it riles me to see how nonchalantly some individuals will suggest social workers simply 'give up' their jobs if they're raising issues about the difficulties they face. This need of having to work to survive means that, while my gut reaction is to tell people to preserve themselves, the reality of work is that you can't just get up and leave the moment you feel you're running on empty.

It would be nice if I could give better advice, but it's hard not to be pessimistic about the future of social work. There are thousands upon thousands of people working in a profession that is restricting them from practising to the best of their abilities and is shutting them down from making real change in the world. All this procedural practice, with social work being performed inside an iron cage of bureaucracy and performance monitoring, is down to a lack of adequate finance. All decisions made by upper-management are driven by money.

This pressure finds its way down to social workers in the bullying culture that I've seen creeping into the profession for the best part of a decade. I worry we've now reached a point where bullying has become a covertly acceptable way of managing social work staff; the pressures to work as efficiently as possible being so great that there is no longer space for reflection, creativity or weakness. This has resulted in a culture where social workers no longer have a space to switch off and constantly worry about speaking openly in their office environment. The outcome of these issues is that we've seen an advancing 'them and us culture', where departments within the same council are constantly fighting one another over case transfers and diminishing resources.

Compounding all of this is the panopticon of perpetual performance management that sees far too many people watching social workers and far too few people helping them. It is little wonder that, in such an environment, we are seeing an ever-increasing number of care proceedings being issued by Local Authorities hoping to find court ordered certainty in an uncertain world.

Looking back over the past thirty years, I can clearly see a correlation between a bullying culture in the workplace and a more punitive treatment of service users. The impact of bullying makes social workers more anxious and in turn reduces their creativity. This lack of free-thinking and a move away from person-centred practice has seen social work became more about pleasing managers and less about seeing to the needs of the people we are there to support.

If social workers are distanced from and scared by their managers, they will become distanced from and scared of their service users. At its heart, good social work is all about building relationships, but a culture of fear is seeing our profession became more about ticking boxes than helping people.

The profession I have given the best of my life to is barely recognisable from the one I walked into all those years ago. Without drastic changes, I dread to think what it will have become by the time my children are as old as me.

Chapter Six: If this is the future of social work, God help us all

I work for a council social work department that is currently being 'supported' by a consultancy firm who have been brought in to help with our 'transformation programme'.

This firm managed to save a lot of money for a council in a different area so, on the promise of 'payment by results', they have been brought in to do the same thing for us. After a month of shadowing social workers and collecting data, they have come up with a plan that they promise will save money and increase production. If they don't save money, they don't get paid.

The stress and pressure that this process is putting on already depleted teams is overbearing. They've brought in weekly meetings where graphs are produced and targets that we must meet are discussed. If individuals aren't meeting their allocated targets, they are taken aside and spoken to. Those of us who are managing to meet targets are having to work until 8pm every night and fitting in report writing on weekends just to keep our heads above water.

If by some miracle a social worker has completed all the tasks they have been set for the week, they are still pulled up about something called their 'throughput' and told that they should be getting through more work than they are. When you are in this vulnerable position of feeling like you're no good at your job, it doesn't help that your manager is telling you "other people are managing" and uses the odd high-performing worker as a stick to beat the rest of you with.

Workshops have been set up for scrutinising cases. These workshops are used to monitor social workers and force us to answer questions like:

Have you used all available free services before looking at formal support?

Are you being risk adverse?

Are your assessments strengths based?

Are you undertaking the best practice you possibly can?

To support this new way of constantly working to meet targets as hard as we can, they have brought in new procedures for our admin staff. Our electronic calendars are now given to admin who are informed when we have new case allocations. They now look at your diary and book visits in your calendar without checking with you first. This is done under the guise of saving us time, but the reality is that it makes you feel like you're not trusted or competent enough to manage your own workload.

That initial contact with people is vital to getting off to a good start with service users, but this new system has ripped that out of our practice. Instead of reaching out ourselves, we have admin sending out letters telling people when we are visiting and just copying us social workers in. It's like booking in a new appointment with your dentist.

There is no acceptance of the complex issues we deal with that take time to unravel, or the need to form good working relationships to bring about positive outcomes for people. Instead we are just told to "get through four assessments this week" or "do these twenty tasks". This isn't social work.

When you are given tasks that need to be completed, they only include defined pieces of work such as assessments in your allotted time for the week. This means that travelling to visits, making telephone calls, completing referrals to other services, and doing our own paperwork aren't calculated as essential tasks. When this issue was raised, we were told "stop answering your phones whilst concentrating on finishing one of your tasks".

Well how is that possible? How many calls do we have to take if we're doing something like waiting for a placement to be found?

We need to be available, we need to be accountable and we need to be able to answer our phones. But in the wisdom of our consultants, we are being asked to take on this new way of working and focus on the 'throughput' of assessments and recordable outcomes. This is all coming at a time where many people are having to reapply for their own jobs too.

What is most upsetting throughout all of this is that there is nowhere in the whole 'transformation programme' where social workers or, more importantly, the people we support, are being given a voice. We are paid lip-service by being included in the weekly performance workshops but, no matter what issues we raise, the blame always falls on social workers and our concerns are ignored.

I'm sorry to rant about all of this, but my best friend committed suicide due to work pressures a few years back and I can see other people who are so fragile around me at risk of going the same way.

We are all so desperate to do a decent job and meet these targets, but the pressure this way of working brings is appalling.

If this is the future of social work, God help us all.

Chapter Seven: Before Baby P

When I first meet Sharon Shoesmith in person, I expect her to be filled with anger and injustice about everything she's had to go through over the past ten years. Made a pariah by tabloid newspapers, sacked live on television by the then Children's Secretary Ed Balls, having a gang of journalists camped outside her house for weeks on end and facing frequent death threats for having 'blood on her hands', Sharon Shoesmith has been put through hell and I imagine that she will be jaded by her travails.

Instead, I find a kind, gentle, funny and softly-spoken woman who is far removed from the "stern, unfeeling and uncaring bureaucrat" Sharon believes she was portrayed as by the national media in the aftermath of Peter Connelly's death. Coming off the back of years of personal academic study into the circumstances surrounding Peter's death and the political storm that followed, Sharon is once again in the national spotlight when I start getting to know her. The difference this time is that she is engaging on her own terms, sharing the lessons she has learned from throwing herself into a forensic analysis of what happened in the years following Friday the third of August 2007, the day that Peter was found dead in his cot.

Peter was only 17-months old on that midsummers day when his little body finally gave out on him, having endured more than fifty injuries over the last eight months of his life. His injuries at the time of death included a broken back, broken ribs, mutilated fingertips and missing fingernails. On one occasion he had been punched so hard in the face that he swallowed a tooth.

Sharon Shoesmith did not break this innocent little boy's back. Nor did she break his ribs, mutilate his fingertips, pull his fingernails off or punch him so hard in the face that he swallowed one of his teeth. She did not deliberately smear this defenceless little boy with chocolate to hide his injuries or display superficial cooperation with social workers as a front for concealing abuse. She was not found guilty of causing the death of Baby Peter.

Yet, when I told my father (a retired coalman whose only knowledge of social work comes from what he sees on the news every evening) that I was going to be interviewing Sharon Shoesmith, the first thing he said to me was "do you have to go to prison to do that?". Such was the focus on Sharon and the infamy surrounding her role in Haringey following the Baby P story, my father had come to believe that she was personally responsible for the death of Peter. He could not for the life of him remember the names of Tracey Connelly, Steven Barker or Jason Owen, but the blanket media coverage of Sharon Shoesmith meant that her name had stuck with him forevermore.

In the days before I meet Sharon for the first time in Leeds, I ask other family members and friends for their recollections on the Baby P case (they all predominantly know Peter by this moniker). Although no-one else I speak to shares my father's belief that Sharon must have been the woman who murdered Peter, every single person recalls Sharon's name as being associated with the tragic death of this little toddler. Somewhat sheepishly, given it is my profession and they know I am writing this book, I also get a few comments about social workers 'failing' Baby P and him being 'let down by the system'.

Nobody could tell me the name of Tracey Connelly, Steven Barker or Jason Owen.

84

Tracey Connelly, Peter's mother, plead guilty to the charge of causing or allowing the death of a child or vulnerable person. After breaching her parole conditions upon first being released from prison, she remains incarcerated to this day.

Steven Barker, Tracey Connelly's lover, was found guilty of causing or allowing the death of a child or vulnerable person. He was later found guilty of raping a two-year old girl, who was also known to children's services. He remains in prison to this day.

Jason Owen, Steven Barker's brother, was found guilty of causing or allowing the death of a child or vulnerable person. He was jailed for six years and is now free, having been given a new identity.

Despite these heinous acts of evil committed against an innocent little boy and the accompanying sentences, it is the name of Sharon Shoesmith that has become synonymous with the death of Peter Connelly.

As I get to know Sharon better, we're eventually able to discuss the infamy surrounding her name and she reveals the impact this continues to have. "Even today, when I'm sat down in the waiting room getting ready to see my Doctor, the receptionist knows not to say my full name or call me Ms Shoesmith when it's my turn to go in. She just says Sharon instead". She considered reverting back to her maiden name following the separation from her husband, but feared that this would be exposed in the tabloid press and painted as an effort to hide from public view.

Even now in 2017, when Peter would have been eleven years old and starting his first year of secondary education, Sharon continues to be lambasted in the national media. The following headlines all come from the past year:

Council chief sacked over Baby P 'cashes in with book'

Furious Piers Morgan slams axed social services boss Sharon Shoesmith for cashing in on Baby P's death

Disgraced Sharon Shoesmith insists she was right not to apologise for Baby P's death because it would have made her look responsible

Sacked Baby P boss' ex-husband exposed as paedophile

Painted as ghoulishly making money from the death of a child, labelled a disgrace for not taking on personal responsibility for his killing and linked to her ex-husband being convicted after being caught with a haul of child sexual abuse images (they had long-since separated by the time his offending had begun) the public shaming of Sharon Shoesmith continues to this day. As this year sees the ten-year anniversary of that sorrowful evening when paramedics were called to a house in North London, finding the blue and lifeless body of a seventeen-month-old boy lying clothed in nothing but a nappy in his cot, it is unlikely that Sharon will ever be allowed peace and anonymity.

With Sharon's role in Haringey and the events surrounding the death of Peter Connelly having been reviewed, scrutinised and criticised in minute detail many times over, I was keen to learn about the human being behind the headlines and the personal journey that carried Sharon to national infamy and beyond. The public exposure surrounding Baby P means that, rightly or wrongly, everybody has an opinion about Sharon Shoesmith and the events surrounding the death of this little boy. Everybody knows Sharon as a professional, but hardly anybody at all knows her as a person, which is what I hope to discover during our time together.

Sharon's road to Haringey is a long and storied one that begins in Belfast, the city of her birth.

From an early age, Sharon had an interest in working with children and helping those less fortunate than her make a better life for themselves. A keen academic, her love for studying and helping children became intertwined as she found a natural outlet for her two greatest passions in education. She developed a special interest in working with children with additional needs after volunteering at a children's hospital when she was fourteen years old. Having crossed the Irish sea and qualified as a teacher in 1973, she took up her first teaching post at a school in Bradford, in the West Riding of Yorkshire.

Teaching in an all-age setting, she began to find an affinity with special education, supporting children with emotional and behavioural difficulties. Recalling those early forays into her teaching career, Sharon tells me "it was all about inclusion" as she found a professional peer group who were as equally passionate as she was in ensuring children had fair access to education services, regardless of their disadvantages or disabilities. Excelling in her teaching role, Sharon moved on to become an advisory teacher and used this platform to encourage mainstream schools to accept children with special educational needs. A great advocate for inclusion, she successfully championed the needs of many children who would have otherwise been denied access to mainstream education.

In 1986, Sharon took what she describes as a "big jump" by moving to a neighbouring council to become their Area Head of Support Services for children with special educational needs. Transitioning from the micro to the meso, she began to have more influence over the direction of support for children with additional needs. In this role, she was part of a movement that saw the council incorporate a model where all children, regardless of their needs or ability, were included in mainstream education and were supported in making the most of their time in such a setting.

Describing the drive for inclusion as a "wonderful programme", Sharon reflects warmly on this time in her life and I get the sense that this is where she was happiest, effectively straddling the fine line between policy and practice whilst making a real difference to the lives of vulnerable children.

Alongside this push for inclusive education, Sharon took a keen interest in the cause and impact of bullying behaviour by children and young people. Taking a somewhat radical approach for the eighties, she helped to introduce a 'no blame' culture when it came to bullying within schools. She shares her belief with me that "the kid who bullies has as many needs as the kid who is bullied" and how she strove to get the schools she was supporting to buy into this way of working. Sharon's view was, and to this day remains, that only by understanding the driving factors behind bullying can we hope to prevent it from reoccurring in future.

Later to be on the receiving end of a progression of brutal and sneering public attacks from a succession of powerful figures in the media and politics, Sharon looks back wryly on an era where she fought so hard to find 'no blame' in bullying behaviour. I wonder if it is her grounding in this way of working with bullies that means she can talk about the public haranguing she received without showing a hint of animosity towards those who subjected her to a public character assassination (although she does at one point make a joke about wishing Ed Balls, who was appearing on Strictly come Dancing at the time when I first meet her, luck by 'breaking a leg').

Two years into her new role and Sharon was faced with the introduction of the National Curriculum. Established within The Education Reform Act of 1988, the National Curriculum aimed to "promote the spiritual, moral, cultural, mental and physical development of pupils at the school and of society". The overall goal of this new universal way of educating children was to "prepare such pupils for the opportunities, responsibilities and experiences of adult life". The Key Stages and performance targets that continue to set the rules of modern statutory education had begun.

Lofty and aspirational goals for the next generation when put down on paper, but the reality of enacting this legislation left Sharon with a feeling that "broadly, these changes worked against children" and not for them. The introduction of new assessment frameworks saw head teachers focusing on league tables and the quantifiable data that would push their schools further up the local ranks. For Sharon, this left little time and space for children with additional needs who needed extra support to "prepare for the opportunities, responsibilities and experiences of adult life". Not only was this shift towards league tables and a more rigid form of education harmful to the children she was driven to support, but Sharon feels a widening gap between students of different abilities harmed all young people. "Inclusion helped all pupils" she tells me "it helped everyone to become more accepting of differences in society and gave a broader experience for all children in school". She was to later experience the fruits of this ideological change to education almost two decades later in Haringey when her push for more citizenship education in the London borough was blocked because of school timetables being filled with subjects that would feed into league tables.

Via working in Trafford as a general education advisor before going on to become a special educational needs inspector in Sheffield, by 1997 Sharon was working as an Ofsted inspector. During the year when Blairmania, Britpop and cool Britannia hit a plateau, Sharon was part of a team inspecting the educational provision at Great Ormond Street Hospital. To this day, it has had a lasting impact on her. "It was a very humbling experience because I didn't think education in there would be a priority for children and parents at first", she explains. "It was very humbling and very moving to see children facing such hard battles, some for their lives, still eager and keen to learn, and their parents still aspiring at such a grim time. The parents in hospital were so concerned about their kids' education and wanting the best for them. The teachers in there were doing their best in difficult and demanding situations".

With an education background herself, combined with close links to health services through supporting children with disabilities and her inspection of hospital settings like Great Ormond Street, I'm keen to find out what Sharon's view of the social work profession was like before she became directly responsible for supporting social workers. Figuring she's faced far more of a grilling by figures such as Piers Morgan and Evan Davies, by the time of our second interview I'm bold enough to come out and ask Sharon "what did you really think of social workers when you were in education?".

Having worked in multi-agency settings throughout those decades, Sharon eschews the cultural stereotype of liberal do-gooders in sandals and chunky sweaters. Instead, she tells me "because I was running units for children with behavioural difficulties, I came across a lot of fostered children who had social workers of their own. There wasn't the same level of animosity and difficulty between different professionals back then. We all worked in partnership to get the best outcomes for children. There wasn't the same type of public negativity towards social workers either. Social workers were just a different type of professional doing a different kind of job to help people".

Given the subsequent media-fuelled public backlash against the social work profession, which she knows better than anybody, it strikes a chord to hear Sharon speak of a more cooperative time where social workers had professional parity with their multi-agency colleagues. The reason it strikes a chord to hear Sharon speak of such a time is that, in my practice at least, it has always felt as if we are at the bottom of the professional hierarchy. On a budgeting level, my colleagues in education and health have financial resources that far outstrip my own. As professional bodies, teaching and nursing associations have far greater weight in their voice and reach than social workers do. In relation to power and respect, police have far more security (albeit with greater risk) and authority in terms of what they can do.

There are reasons for this of course, chiefly that our profession is far younger than those I have unfavourably compared us to and that our workforce is significantly smaller. Those factors don't stop me wishing that social workers were thought of in more positive terms though, or that more people knew what we did on a day-to-day basis and saw the positive outcomes of our work. If you were to walk up to a random person in the street, they'd have a fair idea about what a nurse, teacher or police officer does. Ask the same question about a social worker and you're likely to get a vague response about 'helping people' at best and an accusation that we're 'child snatchers' at worst. Maybe I'm seeing Sharon's description of mutual respect through rose-tinted glasses and that vision is clouded by a haze of fake nostalgia for a time I've never experienced. Maybe I've just got a chip on my shoulder. Either way, there's something mightily appealing about the collaborative working she describes. The irony that Sharon feels professionals may have worked better with one another long before the introduction of legislation forcing us to do so, such as *Working together to safeguard children* (HM Government 2006-2015) is not lost on me.

Just as The Education Reform Act of 1988 was to significantly shape the future of her own profession, Sharon believes the publication of the Butler-Sloss (1988) report in that same year sowed the seeds of public distrust in children's services, the produce of which continues to be reaped to this day.

In 1987, Cleveland County Council comprised of the three post-industrial towns of Middlesbrough, Hartlepool and Stockton-On-Tees. In the previous year, the area had levels of child sexual abuse that were broadly similar with the national average for the United Kingdom. From February to July 1987, suspected cases of child sexual abuse almost doubled. The reason for this sudden and unexpected rise in sexual abuse was put down to the work of two paediatricians, Dr Marietta Higgs and Dr Geoffrey Wyatt of Middlesbrough Hospital.

Over the course of six months, 121 diagnoses of sexual abuse were made by the pair using a new practice called reflex anal dilation. Under extreme pressures due to the massive spike in referrals, Cleveland children's services began regularly using Place

92

of Safety Orders to remove children from their family homes in midnight raids. Such were the numbers of children being taken into care, space in residential homes and foster care ran out. The County Council had to resort to housing children in hospital wards set up especially for them.

The chaos of the situation resulted in worldwide media attention, parents of children taken into care marching and campaigning, and a fracturing of relationships between police, doctors and social workers. In response to the scandal, Elizabeth Butler-Sloss was commissioned to write a report scrutinising what had taken place in Cleveland. Her report resulted in more than 75% of children being returned to the care of their parent's due to incorrect diagnoses of sexual abuse by the two paediatricians (Campbell, 1997).

Although a sizeable number of children would go on to be referred back to children's services at a later date and it would be claimed a decade later that most diagnoses made by the paediatricians were correct (Campbell, 1997) the Butler-Sloss report had a devastating impact on public confidence in the social work profession. The current fear of social workers being 'child snatchers' was forged by the midnight raids on unsuspecting families that saw children whisked away to hospital wards in the middle of the night. The modern lack of confidence in social work evidence was fuelled by the fallout from Dr Higgs and Wyatt's controversial anal dilation technique. The public image of social workers being ineffective and failing children was given credence by the Butler-Sloss report that damned more than three-quarters of the decisions made at the time. For Sharon, the view that social workers were child snatchers who took children on a whim had begun as soon as the Butler-Sloss report was published. She feels we have never recovered from that blow and people have been suspicious of our profession ever since.

Having separated from her husband and with two daughters now in their teenage years, the late nineties saw Sharon throw herself into her inspection role with aplomb. Taking on increasingly more complex and high-profile tasks, she saw herself inspecting education settings such as secure care centres that housed infamous young people who had murdered other children. In such environments, Sharon began to see the aspects of mental illness that drove young people to do such horrible things to other children and gained an insight into the behaviours that fuelled murder.

Coming face-to-face with some of the most troubled young people in our society during her time inspecting secure settings, Sharon was tasked with getting their views on the education that remained a statutory right during their incarceration. Not an easy thing to do, she shared with me how she'd "always try to open up a space for young people so they would be able to share their experiences with me. There was an old saying we used to go by that said if you didn't find abuse in residential settings you weren't looking hard enough".

True to that saying, there were many times when Sharon's inspection work discovered young people suffering in secure settings. She recalls one occasion where a young person disclosed abuse to her late on a Friday afternoon and, following her making calls to the police, education department and Ofsted management, the whole secure school was closed within days. Rampant and widespread abuse was discovered in the subsequent full scale investigation.

The parallels between the position she once held as an inspector and the responsibilities of the hundreds of social workers she would go on to look after in Haringey are clear to Sharon. In both roles, there is a need to find out the truth of a given situation. In both roles, you are faced with the dangers of collusion and disguised compliance. In both roles, the skill of forming effective relationships is key to correctly assessing the strengths and risks you are presented with. In both roles, time is the greatest and scarcest commodity.

That rare and valuable commodity of time is something Sharon knows is needed for engaging those you are working with and reflecting on the information you glean from established relationships. Returning to the skills she honed when working directly with vulnerable young people in secure settings, Sharon tells of how she needed the time to practice and develop those qualities. She had twenty-five years of practice behind her before being in a position where she was working directly with children locked up for murder. Comparing her own professional journey to social workers who can be faced with people who go on to murder their own children within months of qualifying, Sharon tells me how "a lot of social workers have a hell of a lot of responsibility in those tricky situations and don't always have the time they need".

As the 20th Century was ending, ten years of the national curriculum and league tables left Sharon with the feeling that education and social care had drifted further apart than ever before. With teachers increasingly focused on high-flyers, Sharon saw a situation developing where children with more complex needs and those from disadvantaged backgrounds were allowed to drift through their compulsory education before being kicked out into the real world at sixteen. Instead of early intervention and raising aspirations for all, as she had strived so hard to achieve when working in schools herself, she saw a landscape where "we were just saving up and storing these problems experienced by vulnerable young people in schools". Issues that might have been addressed through the education system were untouched as young people left school wholly unprepared, later to be picked up by the criminal justice system, the NHS and social services. The cycles of deprivation allowed to keep spinning, generation after generation.

For all the love and dedication she tried bringing to her role as an inspector, Sharon was all too aware of the fear and dread that she caused when walking into schools. "I realised that there were teachers out there who were scared to death because I would be visiting" she told me. Knowing the negative impact that her inspectors' role was having on a teaching profession she had once been part of began to eat away at her and, over time, Sharon started to dream of pastures new. The end of the line came one day when she was inspecting a secondary school in Liverpool. Observing a young teacher she believed was doing a marvellous job in terribly difficult circumstances, Sharon realised how her presence was only adding to the pressures that the teacher was facing already. Seeing this young woman physically shaking because she was so scared of being observed by Ofsted, Sharon realised there and then that being an inspector was no longer for her.

Those final throes of her time as an inspector highlight an issue that Sharon feels continues to run right through the heart of education. Effective co-working between teachers and social workers has been seen as a holy grail for safeguarding that successive pieces of legislation and professional guidance have attempted to achieve for many years. A young teacher, petrified by the prospect of a damning inspection from Sharon, was solely focused on getting through that visit by Ofsted and pushing her students to achieve the goals she'd been set. She had little time to learn about her pupils' personal lives or take an interest in their wellbeing when the cost of doing so could very well be a poor assessment of her teaching skills. In such an atmosphere, it is little wonder to Sharon that teachers have scant time to commit to effective collaborative work with social workers. With social workers facing similarly pressurised and target-driven cultures in their own workplaces, Sharon feels that barriers to working together are multiplied.

Wanting to go back to working for a Local Authority, Sharon found a home in Haringey through a position with Capita, the business management outsourcing company. Capita had been approached to bring on board a team to help raise the standard of education within the London borough and Sharon was employed by them as the deputy director for school inspections. Taking on a key role in improving schools in the area, Sharon told me how she "loved" her role but that the move to London was a culture shock at first. "I was down in London during the week and then back home on a weekend because my daughter was doing her A-levels and we didn't want her changing schools. Aside from that, it was a very exciting time in Haringey where there was great energy and enthusiasm for the changes we were trying to bring about".

As was to be expected with an outsourced company coming in and telling long-standing education institutions that they needed to improve, Sharon met some initial resistance in her work. This soon changed though, and she recalls the exact moment that she managed to get people to buy into her new vision for the borough. "I got all the head teachers together in a room and I asked them 'can we do this?'. I then asked them 'tell me what it is that's holding you back?'. The questions I posed that day helped people self-reflect and see that often it was their own negativity and attitude that was holding them back". Instead of accepting that negativity, Sharon would instead ask "How can we help you out?" and try to move forward with a proactive approach to resolving the issues brought forward by teachers.

Starting off with the basics, Sharon's priority was to build up the English and Maths skills of all children in Haringey. From this foundation, she then went on to focus on other core GCSE subjects as she pushed her vision that every child in the borough, regardless of background or ability, would be offered the chance of a better life through education. "I was hardly in the office at all" she tells me, "I was out there in schools every single day, meeting with the teachers doing the job and the children being taught in our schools. I relished the challenge and we celebrated achievements together. I used to go out with bottles of champagne on exam results days to show the staff how much I appreciated all they had done for the children of Haringey".

Of all the people she came across in her time as Deputy Director of Education in Haringey (she was responsible for 82 schools in total), one child's story will stick with Sharon for the rest of her life. "The kids' achievements were breath-taking and a lot had the most difficult start to life you could imagine" she tells me. "One child had come to Haringey as a refugee from a war-torn country and when she started at school she could hardly speak any English at all". Some years later, with Sharon then in her role as Director of Education and Children's Social Care Services, she came across that little girl once more as she was out celebrating GCSE results day. The girl who had been exposed to the horrors of war and could hardly speak English when she arrived had just found out that she had achieved A stars across the board in her GCSE results.

Sharon's account of her time spent improving schools in Haringey isn't tinged with hyperbole and the results she achieved aren't exaggerated. Her first four years in role saw educational achievement in the borough improved at twice the national rate for reading and writing (Haringey Council, 2005). By the time she was dismissed in circumstances that the Court of Appeal would later rule were 'procedurally unfair', Haringey was the fourth most improved area in the whole country. The BBC would go on to report that Haringey had the highest proportion of 'good' or 'outstanding' schools in London during Sharon's tenure (Donovan, 2011).

When I raise those achievements with Sharon and bring up the high-esteem in which she is still held by teachers in Haringey, she is typically modest in her response. "Helping children is my life. I've been helping children ever since I walked into that hospital back in Northern Ireland and asked to volunteer when I was fourteen years old. I know nothing else".

Chapter Eight: My time is running out

Today I realised that I have given almost a decade of my working life to supporting children and families. Most of this time has been spent in child protection, looked after or adoption teams. I worked out the other day that in my time I must have supported nearly 500 children and families. I hope that I helped make a better life for some of them.

They say that the burn out rate for social workers is now seven years. I'm three years beyond this and have had to admit to myself that I am getting well past my sell by date. As hard as it is to accept, I should be honest with myself and give in to the fact that my time in social work is coming to an end. I have given my all to this job and sacrificed so much in the hope I was making a difference to the lives of those who needed me.

For a start, my relationship nearly ended last year because I was spending more time with service users than my own family. I guess it's hard to explain to people who don't do this job for a living just how demanding it is. Data protection stops me telling my family just what I'm dealing with and it feels like I keep everything bottled up inside me.

I am also not ashamed to admit that, as well as almost losing my relationship, I have sacrificed my mental health. Eighteen months ago I had a breakdown and my partner had to drive me to the doctors to talk about those feelings I kept locked up deep inside. After much testing, I was diagnosed with stress and depression, all work related. I refused to accept that I was ill at first and kept working to meet targets. I didn't want to let my service users down or be an inefficient worker. But one day I just mentally collapsed and it all came crashing down.

I had dark times during that collapse and I found myself at one point planning to end my own life through overdose of the same medication I was prescribed to help make me feel better. I was medicated to the hilt and was off sick for over six months until I was dismissed by the Local Authority I was working with on medical grounds. I'm happy to say that I am now in the process of reducing my medication, and have just finished my course of counselling, but I know that I will never be the same person I was before the job made me feel this way.

I still have dark times on occasion but these are lessening. That is not me being dramatic, that is just a fact.

I have seen social workers that I have mentored rise above me and continue to fly in their careers. I have been close on several occasions to feeling like I'd worked out the secret to success myself, but I never quite made it. I was too jaded by the bureaucracy and hypocrisy that this job brings to embrace the systematic and procedural ways of working that others used to make a success of their career.

After my time out from work, I thought that it was important to get back in the saddle so I set up my own company to work as a locum social worker. For a while I thought I was on the mend, but after spending time working this way the old feelings returned to haunt me once again. Now those feelings are stronger than ever, I realise that my time in social work is over.

I no longer enjoy the job and each day is a struggle to become motivated. I no longer have the same degree of empathy for my service users and for me that is so difficult as I am a caring person. The body is willing, but the mind is not, and that means it's time to move on. I am not sure what my next steps will be. Part of me thinks that I should just move into another industry, but the other part of me thinks I should stay in this profession and move into a different role.

I once had a vision of starting a social enterprise of social workers to set up a family centre for those on the cusp of care. I dreamed of offering preventative work for families to help address the need for escalation into statutory services. That's what social work should be about for me, stopping children from going into care in the first place and not just getting proceedings done as fast as we can.

Maybe one day I'll return and you'll find me alongside you in the workplace, never knowing that it was my words you read many years ago. Or maybe I'll be gone forever.

Chapter Nine: After Baby P

Sharon Shoesmith still remembers the phone call she received and the voice on the other end of the line telling her "a child has died and he's known to us".

A few days earlier, on the 3rd of August 2007, little Peter Connelly was found dead in his cot by paramedics who had been called to his house in the North London borough of Haringey. He was just 17-months old on that fateful day and had suffered the most horrific abuse from those that should have loved him best. Abuse that his body could endure no longer as his little grip on the edge of life gave out that day.

At the time this harrowing news filtered through, Sharon had been in position as Director of Education and Children's Social Care Services in Haringey for over four years. Sadly, a child being killed by their parent or carer was not unknown to Sharon in her role and Haringey was well-versed in this area due to the murder of Victoria Climbie seven years earlier, at the turn of the 21st Century. Like Peter, Victoria had lived and died within the borough of Haringey. Like Peter, Victoria's life had ended in the most awful way imaginable; her fading memories of this world being burnt with cigarettes, tied up for days on end and being hit with all manner of weapons. She died with 128 separate injuries about a body that was ravaged by hypothermia, multiple organ failure and malnutrition.

Both known to children's services, both living and dying in the London borough of Hackney, both killed at the hands of those entrusted to care for them. Victoria and Peter would go on to also share the tragic fate of being known to the world for the way they lost their lives instead of what they achieved with them. Their deaths would inform safeguarding practices in schools they would never attend. Their short lives would be picked over by academics in universities they would never go to. The pain they suffered would be laid out bare to be seen by a world that they would never get to be part of.

Haringey might have been well-versed in children being killed by their parents and carers, but sadly so was every other area of England at the time of Peter Connelly's death. In the year when Peter died, there were 55 homicides of children where the victim was known to the murderer, 43 being killed by their own parents (Home Office, 2008). In addition, there were 210 child deaths notified to Ofsted where neglect or abuse was either a known factor or suspected (Ofsted, 2008). These statistics bear out the terrifying fact that, in the year Peter died, there was a child death linked to abuse or neglect more than every other day.

Sharon moved to Haringey the year after Victoria had been killed and was well-aware of the public, political and media spotlight on the area. In April 2001, at the same time as she was starting out in her school improvement role, Lord William Herbert Laming had been asked by the Labour government of the time to chair an independent statutory inquiry into the death of Victoria Climbie. Little did Sharon know at the time when she walked in to Haringey, unsullied by the mistakes made before her arrival, that Lord Laming would be doing the same thing only six years later, this time with her as one of the central figures under the spotlight.

Recalling how it felt walking into such an atmosphere, Sharon admits that Lord Laming had the right of it when he hauled services over the coals for multi-agency failings. As well as Haringey, Victoria had been known to Ealing, Enfield and Brent children's services. She was known to three housing departments, two Metropolitan police units and both the Central Middlesex and North Middlesex hospitals. She was also involved with a specialist centre run by the National Society for the Prevention of Cruelty to Children (House of Commons Health Committee, 2003). Despite all this professional involvement, Victoria's case was closed to Haringey children's services on the 25th of February 2000, the same day she died.

"I was shocked at the negativity between education and children's social care when I first came to Haringey" Sharon recalls. "There were lots of trust issues and (in role as education improvement lead) I had a lot of work to bring people together again after the death of Victoria and the Laming report that really dragged the council through it. Schools would pass issues to social workers and expect urgent action, then get frustrated when this didn't happen". The shift away from the holistic care of children by schools and the distrust of social workers that Sharon had first noticed in the late eighties was now bearing fruit in the early 21st Century.

While distrust of the social work profession, catalysed by events such as the death of Victoria and the earlier Cleveland sexual abuse scandal, was an issue, Sharon feels that social workers weren't entirely blameless when it came to effectively working with other professionals during her time in Haringey. "Social workers can be very insular" she candidly tells me. "I saw this when I faced a culture of 'what does she know, she's not a social worker' when I was promoted from a teaching background to become head of children's services".

Speaking to Sharon over sixteen years on from when she first made these observations, I must admit to her that little has changed in the intervening years. I tell her how, in my experience, the social work profession can often feel distanced from our brothers and sisters in education and healthcare; smaller workforces, a vaguer professional identity and negative public image leaving us with a proverbial chip on the shoulder when those from outside our profession attempt to intervene. I hold up the argument about figures such as Josh McAllister (a former teacher, turned Chief Executive of the Frontline social work training programme, with no social work experience) being unfit to take a lead in social work issues as an example of this same discontent rumbling on to this day.

"Yes, social workers really are too insular" she tells me. "It's a protective reaction to the damage that's been done to the profession over the years". The damage that Sharon refers to incorporated her past, present and future at the time when she received that chilling phone call notifying her of Peter's death. She had seen the impact of past media scandals from the other side of the fence when working in education at a time when the Cleveland sexual abuse story rocked the nation. She was presently operating within a culture in Haringey that was significantly shaped by the impact of the fate of Victoria Climbie. Her future was about to be forever altered by what was to come in the aftermath of Peter Connelly's death.

Sharon will probably dislike me using such a term, but she has now become media savvy and remains cool on camera even in the face of challenging questions put to her by abrasive interviewers. The most difficult and indignant of these interviewers have tended to focus on the two key themes of blame and money. They continue to apportion blame on Sharon for the death of Peter and claim that she has feathered her own nest in blood money following his passing, first with a large pay-out following the ruling she was unfairly dismissed (with quoted figures ranging from her earning £600,000 to becoming a millionaire) and then more recently with the idea she is 'cashing in' on his death through the release of her book *Learning from Baby P*. In all the interviews I have seen, she remains the same Sharon that I meet in person and spend hours in conversation with. Softly-spoken, calm, collected and caring.

Her current stance, of embracing the media and engaging with as many people as possible to challenge the negative view of child protection social work, is far removed from the one taken by almost all the people who occupy the senior positions within our profession that she once held herself. Instead of actively embracing the media, we instead tend to see senior figures wheeled out in front of the cameras to firefight in the face of a damning Ofsted report or failings identified during a serious case review. This sees our profession constantly on the back foot as we fight back against damaging stories instead of actively trying to promote the truth that, for every child who sadly dies whilst known to us, there are thousands more whose lives we are making insurmountably better.

Stewart Ewen, a New York-based Media Studies professor, once said "the history of public relations is a history of a battle for what is reality and how people will see and understand reality". I came across his quote a few years ago and it always comes back to me whenever I'm reflecting on the disparity between the reality of social work as I experience it and the image that we see projected in the mainstream media. In the battle for the reality of our profession, frontline social workers are losing badly. We aren't being helped by senior figures who will only engage with the media if they are forced to do so in times of crisis, social workers so scared of repercussions they daren't openly share their views and a belief amongst some journalists who feel they are taking the moral high ground by exposing perceived failings in our profession. Add in the fact that people who feel aggrieved at social work processes are free to share their opinions, yet professionals are bound by data protection from telling the truth, and you have the perfect storm of a profession cowed by the weight of public negativity. Without publicity, there can be no public support, and without public support there is little hope for meaningful change.

The story of Ellie Butler gives a good example of this 'battle for reality' and the impact it can have on both our profession and, more importantly, the lives of those that our work seeks to improve.

Ellie Butler's father, Ben Butler, is a man who used violence, control, intimidation and fear to rule those around him. He has a history of robbery, intimidation, assaults, carrying offensive weapons and domestic violence. In the past, he has admitted that he hoped situations might present themselves where he could engage in violence and believed that violence used to help him improve his mood when he was upset.

When Ellie was just seven weeks old, she suffered a triad of brain and retinal injuries associated with shaken baby syndrome. Ben Butler was convicted of grievous bodily harm and child cruelty, and sentenced to prison as a result. This conviction was quashed upon a successful appeal and Ben proceeded to engage in a media tour to campaign for the return of Ellie to his care. Supported by the convicted sex offender PR-Guru Max Clifford, Ben Butler did the media rounds and portrayed himself as the doting father who simply wanted to care for his daughter. He was the victim of a miscarriage of justice and another wrongfully accused parent who had his child 'stolen' from him by evil social workers.

His story appeared in *The Sun* and *The Daily Mail*, the two best-selling newspapers in the United Kingdom by far, and he also had a live interview on the popular *This Morning* daytime television programme. He seduced the national media with his bittersweet tale of a doting and loving father who was the victim of social work malpractice. He also won his battle in court, with Mrs Justice Hogg commenting of her "joy" at seeing a "happy end" when she returned Ellie to his care.

Eleven months later, Ellie Butler was murdered by her father.

The Local Authority did everything they could to prevent Ellie returning to her father and there was also a heart-felt plea from Ellie's grandfather, who warned the Judge that she would have "blood on her hands" if Ben Butler regained custody. These appeals weren't enough and the battle for reality had been won by Ellie's father. Less than a year after walking out of court, the man described by *This Morning* as a 'doting Dad' would subject his six-year old daughter to a fit of murderous rage before attempting to cover up his monstrous actions by staging an accident; allowing a sibling to find the limp body of Ellie that he had beaten the life out of.

Social workers had lost the first battle for reality in the media because Ben Butler had the stage all to himself. They had then lost the second battle for reality in the courtroom.

Ellie's story doesn't just matter to Sharon because she is another innocent child killed by their own parent. It doesn't just matter because of the media surrounding her situation that went from blindly supporting her father in the face of the best efforts of her social workers, to labelling her father as a monster for his heinous crime. It matters because of the battle for reality that her life encapsulated and the lives that are at stake when this war is lost by the social work profession. Sharon now dedicates her life to publicly supporting social workers and trying to reclaim the narrative of our profession, sending out the message that the excellent outcomes we achieve need to be celebrated, that we need freeing up to spend more time with the people we are there to support. She now routinely does interviews where she speaks of the importance of a new narrative coming forth into the media, one that is owned by those doing the job and not just by those watching others do the arduous work. Alongside these interviews, she spends as much time as she can with social workers and students, telling me that she will accept any invite to engage with our profession, in return for nothing more than her train fare.

Sharon admits to me that she didn't always feel this way and that her current efforts to shed light on the struggles that social workers face are far removed from how she felt when in position as Director of Education and Children's Social Care Services for Haringey. "I have to be honest and say that I would never have voluntarily invited the media into Haringey prior to Baby P", she candidly admits. "The Local Authority culture is embedded with fear of engaging with the press because of a negative media image. Because of this fear, Local Authorities won't dare to push positive social work stories and will only react to stories that are picked up by the media. Local Authorities are constantly on the watch for unwelcome news stories and looking to manage negativity".

The fear of engagement that Sharon admits runs rife throughout the upper echelons of Local Authority management is a vicious cycle, with increasing paranoia about bad publicity restricting positive news stories and leaving journalists without anything good to say about social work. This lack of effort from Local Authorities seeking to meet journalists halfway means that the narrative of our profession is left to those who are free to talk openly without fear of reprisal from their employers. Look at any news story about child protection social work and you will see quotes from family members, BASW representatives, politicians, academics, former service users, campaigners and solicitors. These views are all valid and important, but we are missing the two most important voices, that of the child and that of the social worker doing the job. This dearth of evidence from those out there trying to make the world a better place, as well as the lack of voice being given to people supported by the workers making such efforts, means that the narrative of social work is shaped by the agenda of others. Fuelled by a combination of the irrational paranoia from Local Authorities that Sharon describes and the rational need for protecting children's identities, we are left with a situation where social workers are rarely seen and never heard.

"The culture of blame in Local Authorities means that there is always a demand to know 'who said this' and a need to know 'whose name is on this'" Sharon tells me when I ask her to describe the day-to-day workings of a council beset by fear. "I used to have a whole file about accountability that my personal assistant held with details of who had put their name to what. Haringey was fraught with that negative blame culture. There was always this fear of who would be left carrying the can".

I explore why Sharon felt the need to take such steps and she opens up to me about the culture of fear she found in children's services following her making the step over from her role in school improvement. She reveals that this culture started from the very top of the council and was rooted in the political machinations that social workers so rarely hear about. "The Labour council group had a lot of tension with the Liberal Democrats who were on the rise" Sharon recalls. "This small Labour majority created high tension and filtered down to the rest of us, making for a nervous workforce. There were constant sackings and a massive staff turnover which meant it was difficult to maintain staff. The average employee across the whole Council was taking fifteen days off sick every year when I was there".

Sharon's time as Director of Education and Children's Social Care Services sounds far more difficult than any of her previous roles and, as she recalls the culture of fear that hung over every aspect of her role, I wonder how she kept going for so long in a job that was hard right from the very start. "I was okay with it because I like a challenge and we also had money to try and do good things for the borough. I opened seventeen children's centres during my time there and, for all the issues I faced, in many ways it seemed like a real heyday for children's services. Ofsted told us that we were consistently good and, even in the year Peter died, we had five positive inspections of different services across the borough". She had to fight hard for social workers, facing criticism from councillors that there were "too many kids in care" and questions of "why do you need this budget for the children's services workforce?", but it was a fight she mostly won. Adapting to survive in a culture of fear and blame that she learned to accept as part and parcel of any children's services role, Sharon tells me "I would have stayed there until I retired at sixty-five if I could have".

"Up until the negative Ofsted inspection (following Peter's death) I was liked and valued by everyone I worked with" Sharon explains. "Even with the difficulties of having to engage politically, I had a good reputation and councillors liked me because of the work I'd done with schools in the past. The social work department in Haringey was damaged, vulnerable and on edge, but we were beginning to make progress. I was very keen to improve the life chances for children we supported and we were developing a particularly good record when it came to educational outcomes for looked after children".

The most worrying part of the picture that Sharon paints of her time as the head of Haringey's children's services isn't the culture of fear and blame, the high staff turnover or the political tensions that pervaded through everyone who worked within the borough.

It isn't even the frequent sackings or the rising levels of sickness leave she tells me about that must have left staff languishing in unbearable working environments. No, the most worrying aspect of what Sharon describes is just how normal her experience comes across and how desensitised our profession has become to the toxic conditions she encountered when crossing over from education into social care. The issues that she describes are rampant throughout children's social care to this very day and can be seen across the land. They are the reason why the average social worker in England only lasts eight years in the career (University of Bedfordshire, 2013) our sickness rates are 60% higher than the national average (Morris, 2009) and 20% of children's social work positions remain unfilled (Wainwright, 2016).

Sharon repeatedly uses the word "challenging" when recalling her time in Haringey and it's a term I frequently hear from social work luminaries who continue to move within the spheres of influence that Sharon once occupied herself. You also tend to find it mentioned in job adverts that promise a 'challenging role' or in the soundbites of politicians who offer up platitudes to social workers for doing 'the hardest job in the world'. What you don't hear so much of are solutions to remove those challenges described by Sharon. Instead, we are offered up innovative ways of meeting challenges or making social workers better equipped to cope with toxic working conditions. These fresh solutions to old problems most often involve more restructures, increased monitoring of professionals, changes to training and yet another round of new legislative measures. Sharon isn't too convinced that such approaches are going to make much of a difference and neither am I.

Then that phone call came through in early August 2007 and Sharon would move from trying to cope with challenges that most of us can relate to, to one the like of which has never been seen before. All that she had achieved beforehand would be sullied by her name being dragged through the mud by sections of the national media for the rest of her life. All her hopes for the future would forever be tainted by the unescapable link she would have with a little boy called Peter who she had never even met.

In the aftermath of that phone call, and for over a year after Peter's body was found by paramedics, little changed for Sharon or anybody else working in Haringey at the time. Children dying was a harrowing reality of working in child protection and, with a child death linked to abuse or neglect more than every other day in the year that Peter died, it was something that Sharon and others like her had to steel themselves for at some point during their career. The truth that was never spoken of by politicians but known by Sharon was that, if people are determined to kill their own children, there is nothing that can be done to stop every single one of them carrying through with their evil intentions. Successive reports, reviews, laws, pieces of guidance and innovative ways of working have always failed to prevent every child from being killed by their own parents or carers.

On the 11th of November 2008, just over fifteen months from the day he died, Peter's mother, her partner and their lodger were convicted at the Old Bailey. As their sentences were handed out, reporting restrictions on the case were lifted and the world learned of the terrible fate of Baby P. That night's news reports led with the story of Baby P and tomorrow's newspaper headlines would all focus on the tragic story of this little boy from North London. Pictures of his blood-stained clothes would be viewed by the whole country and the gruesome catalogue of more than fifty injuries he suffered during an eight-month period were laid out in print for all to see. Alongside these heart-breaking details came the revelation that he was seen over sixty times by a range of multi-agency professionals during the last year of his life.

116

Lord Laming, who had chaired the enquiry into the murder of Victoria Climbié and would later go on to do the same for Peter, spoke to *The Guardian* at the time the information was filtering through. "What I had hoped was that Haringey would develop services that would make it an exemplar of good practice. Although our recommendations were not directed only at Haringey, I had hoped that they would be a sufficient stimulus for Haringey to say 'never again'" (Brindle and Carvel, 2008).

Whereas Lord Laming spoke with regret but restraint, the national papers were in no mood for pulling their punches and saw headlines dominated with the word 'failure'. Journalists' ire and thirst for accountability was further increased when Sharon spoke at a press conference hours after the guilty verdicts were handed down to Tracey Connelly, Steven Barker and Jason Owen. Revealing that two of her social workers and one solicitor had received written warnings for their involvement with Peter, Sharon confirmed that this was the extent of disciplinary action from her council and that there were no resignations, sackings or further punishments over the handling of Peter's case. Speaking to the assembled press, she stated "I can only begin to tell you the shock and horror there is across Haringey over this. The very sad fact is that you cannot stop people who are determined to kill children". She went on to add the promise that has become so familiar to those following the deaths of children known to children's services, "lessons will be learned".

Sharon looks back on that press conference as a "complete disaster". Her failure to take responsibility, apportion blame, offer any accountability or reveal that people had lost their jobs was seized upon by the media as Sharon neither saying sorry for what had happened to Peter nor offering any sort of explanation for his

117

death. Her bold but honest assertion that "you cannot stop people who are determined to kill children" went down like a lead balloon and was portrayed as her trying to shirk her duties as the person who was ultimately responsible for ensuring children in Haringey were kept safe. She had the title, she had the wage and she was the public face of the borough that was wheeled out to face the baying press horde, but she didn't take the blame for Peter's death or even offer up a sacrificial lamb who would.

As fate would have it, the guilty verdicts and Sharon's subsequent press conference came on a Tuesday, which meant the day after would see Prime Minister's question time held at midday in the House of Commons. Coming off the back of the international financial crisis which had begun in earnest two months earlier, riding a newfound wave of optimism in the Tories and buoyed by rising polls that would eventually lead him into Number 10 Downing Street, David Cameron sensed a chance to go on the attack by tearing into Gordon Brown and his government for allowing Baby P to die on their watch.

"I want to ask the Prime Minister about the tragic death of Baby P" David Cameron put to his opposite number, Gordon Brown. "This happened in the same children's services department that was responsible for Victoria Climbie and, yet again, nobody has taken responsibility and nobody has resigned. Does the Prime Minister agree with me that the Haringey enquiry is completely unacceptable? It is being led by Mrs Shoesmith who is the council's own Director of Children's Services. Does the Prime Minister agree with me that she cannot possibly investigate the failure of her own department?". David Cameron's opening question of the day placed the spotlight on Sharon and directly called on action from the Government to intervene in her handling of affairs.

Gordon Brown's response acknowledged the shock, anger, sadness and horror sensed by the whole nation because of what had happened to a seventeen-month old boy. He went on to talk about how every child mattered and then raised the fact that a serious set of questions needed to be addressed because of what had happened to Baby P. He revealed how his government's response to these questions about the safety of children on a national level would be addressed by bringing in Lord Laming to chair another review of children's services. On a local level, he shared with the commons that the Serious Case Review had arrived with his Children's Secretary that morning and would be considered in due course. He called this combination of both national and local responses "the right thing to do" and promised further action would come about once both reviews had been considered.

Cameron wasn't satisfied by such a bland and unrepentant response, coming back with further questions that once again placed the spotlight on Sharon. "Let me ask the Prime Minister again about the local review. Sharon Shoesmith, who is carrying this out, said that her service had worked effectively. Isn't it unacceptable that the person who runs the children's services department is responsible for looking into what her own department did?".

Brown's response, reflecting on the workings of Local Safeguarding Children's Boards and the cross-party support this move received as a result of Lord Laming's review, once again failed to assuage his opposite number's interest in Sharon. "I asked a straight-forward question and there's absolutely no answer" was David Cameron's response. Heckles from the Labour Party benches about Cameron's line of questioning being "shameful" saw him interrupted, the speaker having to intervene and remind all present that it was not befitting of their status to see debate over such a tragedy descend into "shouting across the chamber".

Picking up on the accusation levelled against him from the opposite benches, David Cameron started up again by saying "I tell you what is shameful and that is trying to shout down someone who's asking reasonable questions about something that's gone wrong. Let's be honest, this is a story about a seventeen-year-old girl who had no idea how to bring up a child. It's about a boyfriend who couldn't read but could beat a child. It's about a social services department that gets a hundred million pounds a year but can't look after children. That's what this is about".

What he said next was to telegraph the future direction that would be taken following his party's election victory in May 2010. "In the case of failing schools, we take them over". Detailing the fact that a quarter of social work positions in Haringey were vacant and linking this to "another child being beaten to death" Cameron called on the Prime Minister to "consider whether time has come to take over this failing department and put somebody in charge who can run it properly for children". With independent children's trusts now the answer to struggling services in Birmingham, Doncaster, Slough and Sunderland, Cameron's call for this type of action from Gordon Brown was consistent with the path his party would later take when he stood in Brown's position, debating Ed Miliband and then Jeremy Corbyn during his own Prime Minister's question time. Brown remained unmoved by Cameron's' request to consider such a model and uncommitted to giving the assurances he was looking for regarding Sharon's role in investigating the alleged failings of her own department.

Later that day, David Cameron followed up his attack on Labour's handling of the situation with an article in the *Evening Standard* that went even further in his condemnation of Haringey council. He once again focused on Sharon's lack of apology and the fact that nobody had been sacked for the failings that led to Peter dying at a time when he was known to the Local Authority. The

120

day after, Ed Balls, the Children's Secretary at the time, ordered that Ofsted undertake a fresh review of Haringey children's services alongside police and health services. Two days later *The Sun* launched their 'Justice for Baby P' campaign. In just eleven days their petition that sought, amongst other things, the sacking of Sharon Shoesmith, had gained more than one and a half million supporters (Parton, 2014). It was delivered to the Government with a demand that "a price must be paid for his little life" and that "Sharon Shoesmith, the smug Haringey Director of Children's Services, must be fired" (Guardian, 2009).

The following week saw the completion of Ed Balls' emergency report that he had ordered two days after the guilty verdicts were handed down to Tracey Connelly, Steven Barker and Jason Owen. The report found that children in Haringey continued to be in danger and delivered a damning indictment of Sharon's claim from the month before that "there isn't the evidence for anyone to lose their jobs, if there was, that would have happened". Haringey's lead councillor, George Meehan, and the cabinet member for young people, resigned from their positions as soon as the findings of the emergency report were known. Using special ministerial powers from the Education Act of 1996, Ed Balls ordered that Sharon follow suit by sacking her during a live televised press conference.

Over the course of only twenty days, Sharon had gone from a Director of Children's Services to a disgraced public pariah; Ed Balls' unprecedented sacking was followed up by the news that Haringey were officially confirming her dismissal without any form of compensation package in place, save for her pension. Alongside this public shaming of her that would lead to her most commonly being described with the prefixed name 'disgraced Sharon Shoesmith', her fight to prove unfair dismissal via the courts would later show how she faced financial ruin because of her sacking.

I don't dare ask her at the time, because it seems such an unfair question to pose, but after Sharon reveals her experiences to me I can't help but wonder if she ever wishes she hadn't made the move into children's safeguarding, or even regrets the decision to move away from the Northern counties she had spent the rest of her working life in before uprooting to London. She was having to operate in a culture of fear long before Peter was killed and, in our conversations on the subject, spoke of relishing the challenges she faced yet failed to recall any happiness in her role as Director of Children's Services. The memories of her last job are far removed from the champagne celebrations, positive outcomes, success stories and adulation for her efforts that she received in the roles she held in the past. Life for Sharon Shoesmith was very different before and after Baby P.

Shirking the question of regret, I instead asked Sharon if she'd be comfortable sharing the impact that those turbulent twenty days had on her and what it was like living day-to-day in the centre of a public and political storm. "I remember looking out of the window as ITV news was broadcast live from outside my front door" she recalls, as the weight of public scrutiny on her role in Peter's death comes back to her. "For a time, I absorbed the media view of me and it made me lose grip on what I knew to be true. I even remember questioning my own sanity and asking if I had hurt this child myself. I was fighting every hour just to keep myself going. I was very close to a big breakdown. I was very fragile. I was suicidal". Although Sharon tells me how she "managed to hold onto reality again", she recounts a particularly low moment when she looked her oldest daughter in the eyes and asked "did I hurt this child?", such was the impact of the media attention that painted her as being responsible for Peter's death.

Sharon surprises me with her admission that she watched the news and kept up with all the reporting on her. I would have imagined that most people's survival instinct would have kicked in and seen them avoiding such a negative portrayal of themselves at all costs. She drew a line at social media however, with Facebook a burgeoning platform at the time and awash with groups that echoed *The Sun's* call of 'Justice for Baby P'. Her two daughters, adept and savvy with social media, couldn't avoid what was being said online as easily and were exposed to Facebook pages swelling with vitriol directed against their mother.

After the mainstream media and the social media, there came the death threats. A typewritten letter was sent to her home address with a chilling warning that one of her own children would be killed to pay back the debt she owed for allowing Peter to die. She received an email with an attached article called *100 Ways to Commit Suicide*, letters suggesting that she should do the honourable thing by killing herself and pictures of Peter with accompanying messages that she had blood on her hands and he would be 'forever on her conscience'.

The hatred spilled over to her family as well. Her oldest daughter was advised by the police to leave London for a week after she received death threats. Sharon's mother, 88 years old at the time, was tracked down to her home by journalists who were eager to get her insight into what her daughter had done to Baby P. Told that her daughter was responsible for the death of a baby, Sharon's octogenarian mother called her in distress at hearing the news that her daughter was responsible for the killing of this innocent little boy. Not even her youngest daughter was protected, with Sharon telling me how "her hair started to fall out with stress because she was reading all of the social media posts about me at the time".

Jobless, publicly disgraced and feeling suicidal, her family falling apart and losing grip on reality, Sharon feared that she would never recover. At one point she was under so much stress that she was advised by a former colleague to take aspirin for fear the pressure of what she was going through would cause her to have a stroke. As I find out everything that she has been through and how low she once was, I can't help but marvel at the way Sharon now puts herself in the public spotlight and gets up to bat on behalf of social workers. Some people would never have come through her experience alive and many more would have changed their name and gone into hiding for the rest of their lives. Indeed, Sharon was once advised by a press officer to "get out of London, go to Essex, change your name, buy somewhere else to live, get your head down and start over again as there is no way out of this". The Sharon I speak to about these experiences is far removed from the person she describes from Christmas 2008 who was a long way from starting her road to recovery.

Sharon's salvation began when she realised that she was not alone in being blamed for the death of Baby P. Although the media spotlight shone most brightly on her, blame was also apportioned to others from Haringey children's services who were deemed to have had a role in the borough's failings. The names of George Meehan, Haringey council's leader; Liz Santry, cabinet member for children and young people; Maria Ward and Sylvia Henry, two social workers, and their manager, Gillie Christou, were all made public in the demand that people be held accountable for this little boy's death.

Speaking as part of a BBC documentary aired in 2014 called *Baby P: The Untold Story*, Maria Ward would finally speak out about her experiences at the time. "The papers said Maria Ward is the most hated woman in Britain. I don't have the words to describe how awful things became. When I saw 'Blood on their hands,' in *The

Sun headline I just didn't understand it. It didn't take long for me to realise where they were going with the story. People had come to the house wanting to beat me up. It would never feel safe again". Unlike Sharon, Maria lost her appeal against unjust dismissal.

Tracking them via the names of their solicitors that were given in newspaper reports, Sharon reached out to contact Maria, Gillie, their head of safeguarding and her own former manager. They got back to her with encouraging messages of supporting one another through their darkest of times and the hope that they might be able to deal with it better together than they ever could alone. "If I hadn't had them, I don't think I would have come through it" she tells me as she reveals that it was the support of this group of five that gave her the strength to carry on living. "There was such a deep sense of shame that we all experienced, but we realised our anger and shame would eat us up from the inside if we didn't do something about it. We were carrying the nation's guilt and blame for the death of a baby. I we'd have carried that forever, there's no way we could have gone on".

Sharon tells me that the group "still have a strong bond" and she remains particularly close to Maria and Gillie, Peter's allocated social worker at the time of his death and her team manager. She explains to me how they met every month at her flat in London to discuss their respective appeals, how they were being portrayed in the media and the political machinations that were moving and shaping their lives like pawns on a chess board. She was, and re-mains, particularly worried about Maria because she was Peter's social worker. Sharon tells me how "Maria was quite ill with post-traumatic stress disorder at the time" and was struggling to cope with the public haranguing and denunciation of her as a social worker.

Sharon dreams of a day when Maria and Gillie are both back practising as social workers and absolved from the blame that they have both been burdened with. "Gillie still carries more blame that anybody else and she's finding it the hardest to move on" Sharon tells me. "Maria needs support on Peter's birthday and the anniversary of his death", the PTSD she once experienced so badly still lingering over her at times when Peter's memory comes swimming back.

From the beginning of December 2008, when Sharon watched Ed Balls sack her on live television, through to the end of May 2011, Sharon fought a two-and-a-half-year appeal against her unlawful dismissal from Haringey. The battle for compensation was hard-fought and would take her through discovering hidden drafts of the Ofsted report that led to her dismissal, accusations that Ed Balls had sacked her under political pressure and losing her first appeal in April 2010. When she eventually won her case on a second appeal, she felt "thrilled" at the outcome and as if she might finally be able to move on with her life.

Four months after her successful appeal and looking to find answers to everything she had gone through, Sharon started a PhD at Birkbeck University in September 2011. She hoped that a forensic analysis of the Baby P phenomenon would allow her to explore the political motivations and media agenda behind her experiences. The output of her Doctorate would find its way into her first book, *Learning from Baby P*, that was published in August 2016. Just as she had done before in refusing to heed the advice of a press officer to "start over again as there is no way out of this", Sharon refused to go quietly into that good night. Instead, she produced a book that her publisher describes as a dispassionate analysis of the events which followed Peter Connelly's death. Having read *Learning from Baby P* and spent hours in conversation with Sharon, I find it hard to believe that the woman I speak to

126

is the same person who wrote the book. The book is, just as her publisher promised, dispassionate and devoid of the heartrending emotional journey that Sharon describes to me during our time together.

When I put this disparity to Sharon, she explains her motivation behind taking a purely academic approach to her writing and why this was necessary. "Lots of publishers approached me and wanted me to write a tell all book that they could grab headlines with" she explains. "But that would have been all about me and not about the issues raised, or about the fact that a little boy died". In these words from Sharon I find the perfect riposte to the accusations she continues to face that she somehow 'cashed in' from the death of a child by fighting for compensation and then writing a book about it all. If she had wanted to 'cash in', there would have been far more lucrative options than writing an academic analysis of the Baby P phenomenon and releasing it through a specialist educational publisher.

A year before the end of her PhD saw two major events that helped Sharon move further on up her redemption arc. July 2014 saw the release of Ray Jones' book *The Story of Baby P: Setting the record straight*. "Ray's book was a big turning point for me" she says. "I cried my eyes out after reading it and coming to the realisation that somebody else could see the truth of what had happened, the truth that we (those involved with supporting Peter) knew". Jones' book was followed up by the primetime BBC documentary, *Baby P: The Untold Story*. Airing in October 2014, this documentary gave Sharon and Maria Ward the opportunity to tell their stories and set the record straight on what had taken place more than seven years earlier. Although it would never be capable of completely reversing her infamy and public shame, it repaired some of the damage that had been done to Sharon by years of misinformation in the media.

It wasn't long after these two events that Sharon's grandchild was born. She describes to me the impact that this had on her and how seeing a new life brought into the world helped to finally brighten her mood. "Three months after my grandchild was born, I got a strange feeling when playing with them. I wasn't sure what it was at first, but then it dawned on me that it was happiness. I realised that for the first time in years I was feeling happy".

A completed doctorate, a published author and a doting grand-mother who has finally learned to feel happy again, Sharon has come a long way from the day she lost her grip on reality and asked her daughter if she really was to blame for the death of Pe-ter Connelly. With her fight against unlawful dismissal won and en-couraged by a gradually shifting public opinion of her, the woman I meet is far removed from the person who was once told to go into hiding and had to be encouraged to take aspirin for fear that she would have a stress-induced stroke.

What's next for Sharon Shoesmith and where do we go from here? I ask her as our time together is drawing to a close.

In her late sixties and well past the time she would have retired had she remained in Haringey, Sharon has no plans to head off into the sunset and live out her twilight years in peace and quiet. Instead she wants to continue building on the momentum she has gained with the publication of her book and use her profile to try and address the issues that canker at the heart of the social work profession. The issues she speaks of are the same ones that she has seen growing throughout her working life: blame, fear, mis-trust, high staff turnover, burnout and a negative public image. Is-sues that were accelerated by the death of Peter Connelly, where Haringey's perceived failings proved to be the catalyst of what came to be known as 'The Baby P effect'.

The Baby P effect saw a spike in the number of children being taken into care immediately after the story of Peter's death came out in the news. Higher numbers of referrals were accompanied by increased care applications as thresholds for intervention were lowered out of fear that other councils in the United Kingdom could become 'the next Haringey'. The risk-averse culture that Sharon had experienced during the latter years of her own career became ever more apparent across the whole country. At the time of discussing this issue with Sharon, care proceedings are at an all-time high, with 14,591 applications made over the course of the past year alone (Cafcass, 2017).

"The only people who can change things are social workers themselves" she tells me, putting me in a slightly awkward position given that I am a social worker and it feels like she's asking for me to come up with a solution to all our problems there and then. I haven't seen as many false dawns for our profession as Sharon, but I have seen a fair few in my time and can't help but agree with her point that change must come from within the profession itself. Changes that have been proposed through reviews, legislation, refreshed guidance and innovative new models of working have, as yet, failed to bring about any meaningful change for social workers and those that we support. Care applications continue to rise, Local Authorities have been shorn of early intervention services, more departments than ever are being deemed inadequate and social workers continue to burnout *en masse* before leaving the profession in droves.

Just as I'm about to have a go at putting forward my own model for saving the profession that I love so dearly, Sharon saves me from potentially embarrassing myself by setting out her seven-point plan:

- Social workers need to be part of a large independent body that can accurately and passionately reflect the will of the profession.

- Social workers must stop being weak and accepting their given position at the foot of a professional hierarchy that sees the views teachers, health professionals and the police given far more credence.

- Social workers need a focal point or figurehead to band around. They need a campaign or a leader that can inspire and unite them to reclaim their profession.

- Social workers need a stronger voice and better ways of advocating for change.

- The whole profession must try and unite behind a common cause. In-fighting between different areas of practice, arguments between fellow professionals and navel-gazing debates will only hamper us making a real difference.

- Managers at all levels need to get behind these changes and realise that it is part of their role to fight for a better way of working.

- The profession should get better at engaging with the media and telling the story of all the good that is achieved.

On Sharon's last point about the media, we return to Stewart Ewen's advice that "the history of public relations is a history of a battle for what is reality and how people will see and understand reality". Bringing this point back up again, I ask Sharon how social workers can better engage with the media when our livelihoods could be at stake if we are deemed to be speaking out of turn by our employers. "I want to bring together a PR management task-force who can mobilise anywhere in the country to support social workers facing the same kind of issues that Maria and Gillie faced" she explains. "I'm talking with people at the moment about setting up this network who can respond to negative news stories about social work and offer support to people who are being blamed for failures. I'm happy to use my profile and experience to get it going, but I need support from social workers".

With the fallout from the College of Social Work's closure still being felt by ex-members who mourn its missed potential, and social workers continuing to raise concerns about how poorly our profession is represented on the national stage, the time seems right for a movement such as Sharon's to take hold. With the Children and Social Work Bill rumbling on through a game of political ping-pong, proposed accreditation of children's social workers about to be introduced, a drastic cut in agency social work wages (due to tax changes) and a new regulator in the offing, it feels like children's social workers are going through a period of change that has rarely, if ever, been seen before.

In an era where the professional landscape is going through such significant changes and the political debate is dominated by Brexit, the planets seem to have aligned for a grass-roots movement such as Sharon's taking off. Time after time we have heard the words 'lessons will be learned' after social workers have been accused of failing innocent little children who suffered the most awful of ends at the hands of their own parents. Time after time the response has been expert reports and reviews brought about to prescribe changes to the profession. Time after time these traditional political responses have failed to make much of a difference in the world, with social workers still working in toxic environments, more children than ever being taken into care and departments haemorrhaging experienced staff. The same issues of recruitment and retention that David Cameron lambasted Gordon Brown for in 2008 continue nine years later, seven of those years overseen with his own Conservative Party having the chance to make amends.

Sharon has always relished a challenge and listening to her life story taught me just how hard she has fought for what is right. If she can pull off this dream of creating a new network of social workers, dedicated to improving the public image of the profession and supporting those on the receiving end of a hostile media, she has the chance of leaving behind a legacy that will benefit everyone connected to our profession.

Life before Baby P was simpler and life after Baby P was hard. Her life beyond the spectre of Baby P may just reap rewards that see Sharon Shoesmith remembered as somebody who changed the face of our profession for good, once for the worse through no apparent fault of her own, and once for the better through dedicating her retirement years to the betterment of social work for all. As Sharon tells me as we say our final goodbyes before she goes back to babysitting the same Grandchild who taught her how to smile again, "watch this space".

Chapter Ten: The Clown
of Aleppo

'He lived to make children laugh… in the darkest place'

Anas al-Basha, known throughout the world as *The Clown of Aleppo*, lost his life to a bombing raid in the Mashhad neighbourhood of Eastern Aleppo in early December 2016. When his parents fled to safety, Anas stayed behind in his war-torn neighbourhood to offer counselling, financial support and care to many hundreds of orphaned and abandoned children via the Space for Hope charity he worked for.

Mahmoud, his brother, gave his tribute to the social worker by describing how "he lived to make children laugh and happy in the darkest, most dangerous place on this world. All Anas wanted was to bring happiness to the children of Aleppo. I am proud of you my brother. May you rest in peace in a place better than this cruel world".

With 100,000 children under siege at the time of his death, no functioning hospitals, and exhausted food stocks, Anas put himself at incredible risk to try and bring a little hope and safety to the lives of children in one of the most dangerous places on earth. In a place that the United Nations had warned was at risk of 'becoming a giant graveyard', Anas stayed to try and make the lives of the children who lived there a little more bearable.

His supervisor, Samar Hijazi, remembered him as someone who loved to work with children. She told the Associated Press how "he would act out skits for the children to break the walls between them", eventually paying the greatest price for his dedication to helping children.

Anas al-Basha, The Clown of Aleppo, worked in unimaginably horrific conditions to try and protect children from harm.

He gave his life in the honourable service of those who needed him most.

The work he undertook humbles anyone who has ever called themselves a social worker.

His name must never be forgotten.

Chapter Eleven: The singing social worker

Before discovering Edd Donovan, there were only two songs I'd heard that mentioned social workers and certainly no social workers I knew of who performed songs of their own. The first of these songs, *Brenda's got a Baby* by Tupac Shakur, was the lead single from the American rapper's debut album, 2Pacalypse Now. Based on a true story, the song explores the compacting oppressions associated with becoming pregnant at twelve years old and the impact this has on entire communities. Foreshadowing his work to come, Tupac used his lyrics to fight for social justice by highlighting the poor level of support from government services, the baby's father's abusive behaviour and the apathy shown by wider society in general towards the titular Brenda.

Now the baby's in the trash heap balling

Momma can't help her, but it hurts to hear her calling

Brenda wants to run away.

Momma say, you makin' me lose pay, the social worker's here everyday

Now Brenda's gotta make her own way

Can't go to her family, they won't let her stay

No money no babysitter, she couldn't keep a job

She tried to sell crack, but end up getting robbed

So now what's next, there ain't nothing left to sell

So she sees sex as a way of leaving hell

It's paying the rent, so she really can't complain

Prostitute, found slain, and Brenda's her name, she's got a baby

The second, and more recently released, of these songs was *Geraldine* by the Scottish Indie band Glasvegas. The band's lead singer, James Allan, was inspired to write his ode to the profession by a real social worker who quit her job to follow the band around and help sell their merchandise on tour. In an interview with *The Guardian* (O'Hara, 2009), the real Geraldine Lennon had this to say about becoming the coolest social worker in the world:

"I worked for Glasgow City Council's social work department, on the addiction side. It was a thankless job, but very rewarding at times too. You learn very quickly that if you expect people to change their life overnight, you'll be let down. But you learn not to judge. James' sister Denise worked in the same office as me. I think a lot of the lyrics come from her going home and talking about difficulties in her relationships with clients. Usually the only time you hear about social workers is when something's fucked up and has been horrendous. I've spoken to social workers who've said, 'that song gets me to work in the morning', and it was the same for me. Somebody has put value on what we do. When James said he was writing a song called Geraldine, I thought he was taking the piss. When I heard it I was blown away. A lot of tears. It's probably one of the most special things anyone will ever do for me".

I will turn, I will turn your tide

Do all that I can to heal you inside

I will be the angel on your shoulder

My name is Geraldine, I'm your social worker

Released way back in June 2008, *Geraldine* continues to be the last song about social workers that made its way onto radio playlists and into the Top 40 charts. To this day, it remains a firm favourite for many people within the profession and an anthem for the honourable deeds of social workers.

A rap icon who changed the face of his own music scene forever and has gone down in history as one of the greatest hip hop artists of all time. An Indie band that, for a time, were one of the most exciting new bands Britain had produced. Edd Donovan certainly has stiff competition when it comes to writing songs about social work and he's about as far removed from an iconic American rapper and edgy Scottish Indie band as you can possibly imagine. Commenting on his appearance in a tongue-in-cheek manner with his song *Glasses and a Beard*, Edd looks just like how you would expect a folk singing social worker to. More important than his different music styles and more modest ambitions is the fact that Edd is a social worker who continues to work full-time as an Approved Mental Health Professional (AMHP) and Clinical Case Manager. For all of Tupac's struggles with the 'thug life' he advocated towards the end of a career that was cut short with his murder, I can't imagine he ever faced the struggle of having to find a hospital bed at 11:30pm on a Thursday night before preparing for a gig the next day.

"I am I plus my circumstances" Edd tells me when we first start talking, quoting the Spanish philosopher Jose Ortega y Gasset. As I go on to get to know him better, I can't help but think of how fitting a quote that is for a man who is eternally torn between the artistic freedom of his musical passions and the increasingly rigid procedure of what he does for a living. He is the artist that follows his dreams as well as the social worker defined by his circumstances.

Edd was born in St Helens, on the fringes of Merseyside, and although his scouse accent has mellowed with age and distance, it lingers in both his speaking and singing voice. Growing up, his circumstances were defined by being raised in a household where art wasn't valued and music wasn't celebrated. He wasn't given the advantage of privilege, encouragement or an early introduction to music that many of his contemporaries on the folk scene enjoyed. He describes himself as being "without ambition in school" and, like many young men from Northern towns in the eighties, feeling a "little bit lost" as his compulsory education was drawing to an end and leaving him with no real plans for the future. Before I can start feeling too sorry for him, Edd tells me that he was happy with his lot and a "bit of a party animal as a young one. I left school without a job lined up or any direction, but I enjoyed it" he recounts. "I was without direction, but that didn't make me a lost soul".

As the eighties turned into the nineties, Edd got into the burgeoning Manchester music scene as bands like the Stone Roses and the Charlatans began to take off. "They were the first bands that seemed like us" he tells me, "that looked like me and my friends and came from the same kind of backgrounds we all did". At the same time as this first wave of Indie bands that would go on to define the musical landscape for the next decade was coming out, dance music was crossing over from Ibiza and into the mainstream youth culture of the North-West. In the years before The Criminal Justice and Public Order Act 1994 put an end to it all, illegal raves were plentiful. Speaking with the chuckle of a man who has enjoyed a misspent youth and come out the other side to tell the tale, Edd says "it was a good time to be a teenager".

Aged eighteen in 1990, Edd took up the offer of a hotel management course on a whim and moved south to Cheltenham. There was nothing particularly appealing about the course or enticing about the location, but it gave him an opportunity to get out of

St Helens and see a bit more of the world. Just as directionless and demotivated by studying as he had been in his hometown, Edd was kicked off the course before the end of his first year. He'd made good friends in the area so, rather than heading back home with his tail between his legs, decided to put down roots and signed up at the local dole office.

"Everyone I knew in Cheltenham was into music and every other student at college seemed to have a guitar" Edd tells me. "I joined in, got a guitar, and taught myself how to play. As soon as I learned a couple of chords I started to find writing came naturally to me. My musical tastes were maturing from the baggy sound of Madchester as I began to get into Bob Dylan, the later Beatles records and Simon and Garfunkel. My writing reflected those new genres and became quite psychedelic". Most of those early songs were a snapshot of his life as an unemployed college dropout, far removed from the married professional family man he is now and impossible for him to sing with any sincerity these days. Some of the less personal songs he penned in his early adulthood have stayed, with melodies and lines from his fledgling efforts finding their way into *The Stone* and *We are the Wandering Moles* on his first album, released over twenty years later.

"I don't sing as freely as I did when I was a young man", Edd tells me during our second interview session together. Using a beautiful turn of phrase, he describes his feeling that "age has suppressed me with experience" before telling me how his music now combines "the melody of youth with the lyrics of wisdom". After hearing him say this, I will later go back and listen to his albums again to pinpoint what he's talking about. Framed by what he has told me, I find that the jangly sprightful guitar melodies, reminiscent of The Byrds and Stone Roses, jar with hard-hitting lyrics that explore some of the darkest issues of human life.

Edd's candid and honest nature astounds me. In a profession that is fraught with risk-aversion and filled with people so scared of causing offense that most daren't offer any personal views at all, he is a breath of fresh air. "I frequently used recreational drugs and alcohol for years" he openly admits. "It went hand-in-hand with spending many years unemployed and aspiring to very little in the way of a career. For a long time I didn't recognise I needed to change. However, such a lifestyle began to take its toll and I became low in mood, lacked self-esteem and suffered with anxiety".

After five years of being unemployed and with his mood at rock-bottom, his local job centre sent him on a course that was to change his life forever. "My social working days began when I was given the opportunity through the Princes Trust volunteers to provide support at the Vitalise Sandpipers Holiday Centre in Southport" Edd explains to me (Vitalise was a national charity providing short breaks and respite care for people with disabilities and their carers). "This was a powerful experience and had a profound impact on my life. I realised that I had something to offer people less able and fortunate than myself and realised I could support and care for people as a career".

"Caring just seemed to come naturally to me and I remember feeling very emotional and warm after seeing the impact I could have on other people. It was a different and new feeling for me to give to other people like that and I embraced it. I remember crying afterwards because I was so emotional about what had happened and thinking that maybe there was something out there for me to do with my life after all".

Finding a direction and purpose that had evaded him for so long, Edd used a member of staff he volunteered for as a reference to start applying for his first paid employment in social care. "Every other job had seemed like part of a capitalistic rat race before then, but that experience made me realise that I didn't have to be redundant any more". He found his first paid job in a residential setting for the elderly as a care assistant. Edd would then move into mental health, working as a keyworker in a privately-run rehabilitation home for people suffering with mental health issues and acquired brain injuries.

His musical passions lying dormant as he settled into the working life, Edd found a steady and settled life in care. "However, as time wore on I felt I needed change, but couldn't see much opportunity other than managing such a home, and that wasn't for me" he explains. Fortunately, fate was to intervene once again when he bumped into an old colleague from his first job in care who had just completed her diploma in social work. Having never really considered it as an option before- still burned by his last ineffective dalliance with education- his interest was piqued by how positively his friend spoke of the course. When she went on to inform him that his financial concerns might be allayed by a bursary that was available to study full-time for a qualification, he was sold on social work.

Less than four years later he completed a social work degree with the University of Gloucestershire and qualified in the summer of 2007. Poetically returning to where it all began, he worked for the Princes Trust Volunteers for a short while before landing a statutory social work position for the NHS in a Community Mental Health team. He remains in the same field of practice to this day, going on to gain a further qualification so he can now work as an AMHP.

Edd and his partner's first child, a boy, was born during the final year of his degree and they had another child, this time a girl, two years later. Shortly after the birth of their daughter, his partner became ill. "Due to those family issues, all music was put on hold for a long time. I've always put my family first and am immensely grateful to have been fully involved in those precious early years". As I hear Edd telling me about those 'precious early years' I can't help but feel a pang of regret about my own family and the tough decisions I have had to make in terms of my work/life balance. There are far too many nights where I've missed my daughter going to bed because I've stayed back at work to make sure visits were done within timescales or assessments were filed in time. The children I had to visit weren't at immediate risk and the assessments would have made no difference if they'd been filed a day later, but making sure I ticked those boxes kept up my reputation as an 'efficient' social worker. I know I'm far from alone in sacrificing my own family life in the line of duty, so maybe there's something most of us can learn from Edd's decision to put his family first. For the rest of the week after hearing Edd speak these words, I work through my lunchbreaks so I can get home in time to read my daughter a bedtime story.

After five years as a social worker, with his partner's health improved, his son in school and his daughter not far off going herself, Edd found the space to start making music a bigger part of his life again. "There was a musical promotion night at a little folk club in Cheltenham I used to go to. Some friends knew that I played and encouraged me to go along, so I asked if I could get up and do a few songs. It went down well and I remember getting a real buzz from being up on stage. That started me off doing the occasional open mic night here and there". Every time he got up on stage he felt his passion for music growing as the melodies of his youth mixed with the lyrics of experience he was now laying down as a father, partner and social worker. "I fed off the audience in those early days" Edd recalls. "My family and friends encouraged me, but hearing positive feedback from a room full of strangers was very different to getting it from people who knew you and might not want to cause any offence. I'd never really been a confident person before, perhaps that's what attracted me to drinking when I was a younger man, but feeding off the positive vibes from a crowd responding to my songs made me believe in myself and that I was doing alright".

With growing confidence that the melodies he'd strummed in a college bedroom during his teenage years and the lyrics he was writing in the back of his notepads as a social worker in his forties were finding an audience, 2013 saw Edd thinking "maybe I can get this music together. I started keeping my eye out for an opportunity to get my music out there and noticed a local competition to record a CD with a music publisher in the region". Entering the competition and winning, Edd bumped into a woman in another band who was listening in to the songs he was singing. "She heard my songs and said she loved my stuff. She asked if she could sing with me sometime and also if she could pass my music onto her husband, a local record producer".

Edd had stumbled into the caring professions due to a chance decision by his job centre to send him on a Princes Trust course. He had wandered into social work by a lucky encounter with a former colleague who'd taken that path herself and encouraged him to do the same. Fate was once again playing a part in Edd's life, this time directing him into the arms of Paul Arthurs, who would go on to produce his records, and Chads Bradbury, who would put in the finance to launch the Paper Label recording company, using Edd as the vehicle for the enterprise.

In stark contrast to the likes of your X-factor winners who might have a pretty smile and a great singing voice, but no creative talent or song writing ability, Edd had twenty years of material to draw on when he entered the studio with Paul and Chads for the first time. Even in those fallow years when he had distanced himself from performing to focus on his family and career, Edd told me how there "wasn't a day that went by when I wasn't thinking about music or lyrics". Ready to record what would become his debut album *Something to Take the Edge Off*, Edd needed to find a band to give his music the depth it deserved.

"In the middle of a drunken jam many years ago I started chanting 'we are the wandering moles' and it stuck with me. Moles are underground creatures that go about their business in an understated way and operate on the fringes of the British animal kingdom. It's also a socialistic term that seemed to fit well with my political beliefs" (the *Red Mole* was a Marxist newspaper from the 1970s). Pulling together a band of friends and connections from the local folk scene, Edd called them his 'Wandering Moles' and his drunken jamming found a home in the name of his new band. That same jam also crystallised into the ethereal song *We Are the Wandering Moles*, the opening track from his debut album.

Being a huge fan of music but in no way musically gifted myself, it astounds me when Edd reveals that *Something to Take the Edge Off* was recorded in one night. That something so fine could be crafted in such a short space of time is hard for me to believe and I ask Edd just how on earth it was possible. He puts it down to a combination of the more than two decades of experience that led him into the studio that evening and the skill of his Wandering Moles. "I'm a singer songwriter at heart but I've always liked to be part of a musical community" he explains, harking back to the musical community he found in college as a teenager and the influence that had on the rest of his life. The backing of the seasoned Moles alongside the care given by his producers Paul and Chads saw the music come easily. I try to inject a little bit of social work

144

humour by lamely calling it a 'collaborative multi-agency team effort'. Edd does the decent thing by faking a chuckle.

There are two songs on Edd's debut album that particularly resonate with me: *House on Fire* and *the Social Worker*. Although much of what he writes is inspired by his experience as a Social worker, these two songs have special meaning for me because of the way they expose the difficulties of those we support in the job that we must do.

About time I got out of here, wonder what life's like on the other side
Been a prisoner of my life, been a prisoner of my own mind
Tell me what did I do wrong to be treated like a lowlife
I've been living on the back of your hand

You may ask, how do I still carry this smile
When you live in a house on fire

Been kicked, smacked, much everything
Seen glass fall in my direction
Seen my dinner decorate the wall
Seen the devil hide behind Dad's eyeballs

You ain't my real Dad but I'm giving all the love that I have
I've been living on the back of your hand

You may ask, how do I still carry this smile
When you live in a house on fire
The curtains close on a smoky room

I don't know what to do
My body shakes every time he moves
I lie awake, I feel confused

I long for the day he will approve
I long for the day he'll love me too

And now my Mum won't get out of her bed
She says it's my fault she can't kill herself

Tell me what did I do wrong to be treated like a lowlife
I've been living on the back of your hand

You may ask, how do I still carry this smile
When you live in a house on fire

Tell me how do you carry this smile
When you live in a house on fire

House on Fire- Edd Donovan

Taking inspiration as well as the title from Andrea Ashworth's book *Once in a House on Fire*, Edd began to pen this song after being asked to read Ashworth's memoir as part of his social work degree. Focusing on the experience of living with a violent stepfather, Edd's song will be familiar to everyone in social work, with the devastating impact of experiencing domestic abuse hanging over every aspect of our profession and significantly harming many of the people we support. He also reflects on his own childhood experiences in this song, sharing with me how one of his earliest

146

memories was seeing his own father throw a plate full of food against the wall in a fit of rage. "The song allowed me to put a little bit of myself in there but to hide behind the title of the book" he explains.

Edd moves beyond that uncomfortable memory from his early years and laughs when he tells me how the assignment that he wrote about the theme of childhood risk versus resilience contained in *Once in a House on Fire* barely passed. "I wish I could have submitted the song instead of the assignment" he lets me know. The song that came out of that mediocre assignment would eventually find its way to Andrea Ashworth herself. He tells me how "Andrea wrote me a beautiful letter after listening to the song. It was the greatest reward I could've hoped for". That recognition and the legacy of putting out such a touching song certainly seem better to me than bumping his mark up from 48% to 60%.

I am a social worker, I know not where I'm from
I guess I'm just a means to an end, I make a friend and then I'm gone
Yes, I'm a social worker and a singer of songs
I am a jack of all trades my friend, you might guess, a master of none

I am a social worker, by accident or default
Now I'm part of a system, of a machine that rages on
Damned if I do, damned if I don't
Damned if I will, damned if I won't

I am a social investigator, don't like what I find
But it takes a social worker, it's a state of mind
I am a social caretaker, a remedy of kind
I am a social medicator, I'll give you something if you like

147

Damned if I do, damned if I don't

Damned if I will, damned if I won't

I am a social lubricator, I'll fit you in best way I can

I might even bend a few rules for you, but you don't tell them if they ask

I am a social special agent, I serve to protect and control

I'd like to give you more responsibility, but In the end I'm responsible for you all

Damned if I do, damned if I don't

Damned if I will, damned if I won't

Damned if I do, damned if I don't

Damned if I will, damned if I won't

The Social Worker- Edd Donovan

Damned if I do, damned if I don't. The recurring line from this song is something said and felt throughout the entire social work profession. It was those eight words, that say so much in such a short space about the pressure of being a social worker, that were the inspiration behind Edd penning this song. "Damned if you do, damned if you don't. Those words stuck with me and I remember having this idea that I wanted to base a song about what I did for a living around them. But it was very hard to write the song off that hook alone and it took me a long time to arrive at the finished article. I didn't want to mess it up because it was such an important song. There was a lot of work that went into those lyrics because, as a social worker myself, I felt I had to do it properly and do right

148

by my profession".

In writing and recording *Born to Run*, Bruce Springsteen set out to write the greatest rock and roll song of all time. Coming off the back of two albums that hadn't sold well upon initial release (their true genius only being noticed retrospectively), Springsteen knew that this was his final chance at making it as a rock and roll star. *Born to Run* was to be the title track from the album that would make or break him and he had to get it right. He wrote, wrote and wrote again, re-recording every track until it was just how he had heard it in his head, until his *magnum opus* was complete.

Although I can't fairly compare Edd Donovan to Bruce Springsteen (sorry Edd, I love your music but there's only one Boss), if you're setting yourself up as the one and only singing social worker you must make sure that your song about social work is up to scratch. Just as Springsteen did with *Born to Run*, Edd worked and worked on *the Social Worker* until it was ready to go. Drawing on his first-hand experiences as a practitioner and the dilemma to intervene or not that is experienced by social workers all over the world, Edd might just have gone and produced the greatest ever song about our profession. It is his *Born to Run*.

Springsteen didn't have a wife while he wrote his first seven albums and had no children until he had eight under his belt. Edd alludes to this point himself when he wonders about his own musical heroes "as for Dylan and Lennon and such song writing icons, it would be interesting to see what they would have written had they had to raise a family and hold down a job whilst keeping a music career on track". Instead of *Strawberry Fields* we might have had 'Best Interest Assessors Forever'. In the place of *Knockin' on Heaven's Door* we could have had 'Knocking on Clients' doors', a whimsical ditty about repeated failed visits to a hard to reach service user.

We laugh and joke about the prospect of John Lennon undertaking a mental capacity assessment whilst declaring that he is 'the walrus', but the cold hard truth is that it can be bloody hard to hold down any sort of personal life when working full-time as a social worker. Balancing family and work commitments is difficult enough as it is, but throw an artistic pursuit into the mix and things can start to get nigh on impossible. Edd acknowledges this when he tells me "achieving all this with my music at the same time as a full-time social work job has been tiring and stressful to say the least. When I was younger I took less risk pursuing my musical ventures and focused on a foundation of securing work and raising kids. But now I'm a little older it feels like I can take a few more risks and I'm now starting to reap rewards because of it. I've created something that I think people will find beautiful. I know I do. You can always find the time to write if it's something you're driven to do, like any passion in life".

Something to Take the Edge Off went down well- receiving glowing critical reviews, steady sales and airtime on national radio shows. After two years of touring folk clubs and popping up at festivals all over the country, he followed it up with a second album called *Making Mountains* (Vol. 1) in June 2016. His sophomore album sold even better and saw tracks picked up by BBC Radio 6, whose DJ Tom Robinson called it "Summery alt-country to gladden the heart".

During my last discussion with Edd, in late spring 2017, he is preparing his touring schedule for the summer that will see him performing material from both his albums all over the country. "Touring is hard as a working artist" he lets me know. "After a gruelling day at work you have to go home and find the energy to get up on

150

stage and perform". I ask Edd if his moonlighting as a successful folk artist has ever impacted on his job. "No, it's never impacted on work. I've never been off sick or late because I've exhausted myself on stage. At first, I was a little wary about letting the people I support know what I did in my free time but then I realised that I had nothing to hide. Being a good social worker means accepting that you're part of a community. Because I live in the same community I work and perform in, I wanted to share what I did with the people I support. They've all responded positively and some have even offered to buy CDs or come along to gigs. I also think it's improved me as a social worker. When you succeed in your personal life and feel happy, it makes you better at your job".

Edd's point about happiness in his personal life and happiness in the workplace going together strikes a chord with me. Not only have I heard the story of thousands of my fellow social workers' personal lives being ruined because of extreme pressures in the workplace, but I've experienced the vicious cycle at times in my own life too. Overcommitting to your job leaves you no time to spend with your loved ones or on your passions. In turn, this leaves you with little opportunity to recover from the rigours of your work and further compounds the pressure that you're under. In the end, you either get out or burn out.

Edd knows that he's a rare breed amongst his fellow social workers for holding down a job in the same team for almost ten years. I add to his point about being settled at work by telling him that he's also one of the few people I've met during my travels that has nothing bad to say about his job. Reading about how hard some of his fellow professionals have it in their jobs, he does feel lucky, but he's seeing changes creeping into his own area of expertise that he fears threaten the role that he knows and loves. "I've seen a lot of changes since I started. The decline of the last remnants of the institutions. The rolling out of personalisation. Care in the

151

community. All those things offered much promise but these days that promise looks like it might be slipping away".

"The end of institutions has now come full circle and less local support services means that care in the community has been replaced by people feeling isolated in their own homes. There are no community services these days and less support just increases this isolation. It's made worse by society getting more stressful as a whole. Personalisation has manifested into a system where social workers are having to bend over backwards to identify every single need a person might have, then tie those needs down into an hourly rate and a business model. People don't fit in to business models and humans are more than an hourly rate".

Working in a multi-agency team alongside health staff, Edd is also worried about a loss of professional identity. "Social workers are being squeezed out of the mental health profession. We struggle to find a voice in mental health services because most of the managers come from a nursing background. This sees the medical model of intervention taking precedence and there's a shrinking focus on the social model these days. I love my job and the responsibility I'm given to help people, but I know the model I use as a social worker is expensive. The social model of recovery is folding in other parts of the country and I don't know how much longer my team will last".

Edd's such a cheerful and friendly guy that I don't want to say goodbye to him on a sad note, so I pick up on his talk of social models and use it as a spur to end on a high. Plucking out the miracle question and hoping it doesn't sound too cheesy, I ask him "where do you want to be in five years' time?". His first plan is to record *Making Mountains* (Vol. 2). With the songs already written and ready to go, it's simply a matter of finding the time to get

152

the Moles back together again and return to the studio. Once this summer's touring is out of the way and that album is recorded, he wants to focus more on the worldwide social work community he is part of.

"Social work has needed a more positive image for a long time. We should be putting out a brighter and more optimistic message than we've managed to so far. It's time we were getting some media attention that changes the stale old story of social workers letting people down. We could at least try and get our profession a better public image than it currently receives. I think I could go a little bit of the way towards helping change the image of social workers by getting my songs out there to a wider audience. I feel a lot of people would strongly resonate and connect with what I'm singing about and I could help shine light on our undervalued community".

Lofty ambitions from Edd, but he's not being sensationalist when he talks of the negative press surrounding our profession. Reporting on social work continues to be dominated by a narrative of failure and primarily focuses on child protection workers, almost wholly disregarding the multi-faceted nature of other roles such as the one that Edd performs. Music has the power to shape culture in a way that no other artform does and has significantly shaped the modern world. Just as bands like the Stone Roses and the Charlatans resonated with Edd as a teenager because they came from the same cultural background as he did, maybe Edd has a shot at shaping our profession with songs of his own.

To paraphrase David Bowie, I don't know where Edd will be going from here (other than Bath, Bristol and Stratford-Upon-Avon as part of his summer tour) but I know it will be interesting. The singing social worker and his wandering moles on a quest to change

the image of a downtrodden profession sounds so fantastic it just
might work out.

Chapter Twelve: My wife the social worker

The love of my life,

I wish I had the strength to tell you this in person and to let you know just how much I adore you for all that you bring to my world. You truly make my life complete and there is not a day goes by where I do not count myself blessed to have found you. As we have grown older together and you have given me a family, the words read out by your brother on our wedding day ring ever more true.

"Those that truly love have roots that grow towards each other underground, and when all the pretty blossoms have fallen from their branches, they find that they are one tree and not two"

We are one tree where yours are the roots that make us strong and bind our family together, holding us firm throughout any storm that weathers us.

Even though you are so strong and wild and spirited and everything else that is beautiful and free in the world, I have seen a change come over you in recent years that ebbs away and withers you. At first, I thought it was a phase, then I thought it was just what happens when you hit your mid-thirties and then I blamed myself for not being the man you deserved.

Then it dawned on me.

You no longer wake with the same enthusiasm to make the world a better place that you used to. In days gone by you'd go out into the community with a dream of making a difference but now that optimistic talk of change has been replaced with a resignation that you're merely treading water.

In the past I'd get text messages and emails from you at work to let me know how your day was going or make plans for the night. Now it seems like you feel guilty for taking the time out to get in touch with me or you simply don't have the time.

You'd once come home talking enthusiastically about your day but now it seems like you'll do anything you can to avoid talking about work. It's great that you want to ask me and the kids about our days, but sad that you're so keen to forget yours.

I know what you do at work lingers in your mind long after you've finished for the day. I know that the things you see and what you must do lay heavy on your heart.

It's like you find it hard to live in the present and enjoy the moment these days because your mind is always on something you need to do in the future. Even when your manager isn't texting you on your days off or you're replying to emails late at night, I can see that you carry the burden of your job with you at all times.

For years, I've stood by your side and watched this change come over you and I worry where you will be if I stand silently by your side for many more.

You are so strong but I think the cracks are starting to show.

Your mother asking me if you'd ever thought about speaking to our family GP about depression last Christmas when she'd had a few too many sherries.

The light coming back into your face after our long holiday this summer.

Seeing your smudged mascara and knowing you've been crying at work again.

I worry so much that these people you work for will keep taking from you until there's nothing left of you to give and then, like all those people you tell me about who go on the sick at work and are forgotten about, you'll be a shell of the person you once were.

I'll be there to pick up the pieces and put you back together, but it shouldn't have to be like this my love. There is more to life than your job.

You are not just a social worker. You are not just there to do what the system demands of you. You are more than what you make a living doing.

You are a mother, a wife, a daughter, an aunt, a friend, a cousin and a neighbour too. You are more than just a job title and every-thing about you that makes you so special and unique is being taken from you by the demands of your job.

You're now so worried about all those stories of other social work-ers being struck off that you don't even dare post your political views online these days and have to use a fake Facebook name, which means it's taking your personality as well.

I know being a social worker means a great deal to you, but is it worth having to give up so much of yourself in return?

I feel so guilty for thinking this way, let alone writing it down, but I have to let you know it's time to take a break.

You've always been so keen to save others, but now it's time to save yourself.

I hope you read this and know it's meant for you.

Come back to us my love.

Chapter Thirteen: Thoughts from a foster carer

A few months before I got to know Martin Barrow, I did a little bit of research into foster care as part of an article I was planning on financial incentives for taking children into care. Sickened by the perverse fallacy that social workers were under some sort of financial incentive to 'steal' children from loving and caring parents, making up lies to see through our wicked agenda, I started looking into the true costs of the care system. Even after all that I had seen from care proceedings during my own work safeguarding children, the figures were astounding.

Far from making any sort of money from 'stealing' children, the cost of taking a child into care was astronomical. When you factored in every outlay that the state made in the whole process-right through from social work wages, to legal aid fees paid out to solicitors and barristers, court costs, specialist assessments, pupil premiums, care packages and foster care allowances- each child being taken into care was costing the state hundreds of thousands of pounds. As well as blowing the argument out of the water that me and my fellow social workers were making up lies to get our adoption bonuses (so the cash that we make for taking kids is coming from the same government who have frozen our wages for ten years?), it showed me where the money spent in the process went.

In terms of an hourly rate for involvement with children who need to be taken into care, the largest slice of the pie went to the judges, solicitors, barristers, specialist assessors and expert witnesses involved in the legal process of seeking a care order. Perhaps it won't come as a surprise to any of you that the smallest piece went to the children themselves and the foster carers who would be given the responsibility of building their lives back up.

The adverts that seek to recruit foster carers probably don't help with the falsehood that they are well paid. They understandably try to attract people into fostering with images of happy smiling children and tempting financial packages. However, when you take a proper look at what foster carers receive, given that it is a 24-hour a day job to raise children, it can work out at as little as 60p an hour.

"It's even less than that" Martin Barrow tells me when I raise this point with him, "being a foster carer costs us far more money than we ever receive in return". But it's not about the money for Martin, it's never been about the money. There's a tired old saying about social workers which goes 'we're not in it for the income, we're in it for the outcome'. I've used that line occasionally in the past when attempting to show the rewards that come from making a difference in the lives of vulnerable people. However, as the years have gone by and I've seen social workers continue to be overworked and underpaid, I've veered away from repeating that saying for fear of devaluing the worth of our profession. It suits Martin though. Being a foster carer isn't a job for him, it's a calling. He isn't in it for the income, he's in it for the outcome of taking in vulnerable children and showing them the love and care that's eluded them in the past.

Martin and his wife Lorna's love story, and subsequent journey into foster care, is a long and complicated one that begins with each of them at opposite ends of the world. Born and raised in Peru, Martin's mother passed away when his sister was only nine months old and he was just a young boy himself. The loss of their mother hung over the children and added to what Martin tells me

160

was "not the happiest household" to grow up in. "My Dad had a quick temper that was made worse by the loss of Mum" he tells me, before adding "I had to grow up quickly". At the same time as Martin was experiencing his own difficult start to life, his wife was on the other side of the world suffering a similarly turbulent childhood in Australia.

"Lorna had a very difficult start and is aware of how hard life can be for children. Her parents emigrated to Australia when she was a child and, soon after the family arrived, her mother and father's marriage started to fall apart. Isolated from her friends and family, her mother suffered at the hands of her father. It got so bad that she hatched a plan to flee, started secretly saving up money and fled the country when she'd saved up enough to bring herself and the children safely back home to England".

Aged sixteen and seeking freedom from his father, Martin left home and found work in a local factory. Speaking to him now, it's hard to believe that a man who would go on to hold the prestigious position of news editor for *The Times* started his working life with two years spent living in digs whilst employed in a Peruvian factory during the late 1970s. Just as he and his wife's childhoods would go on to give them a little more insight into the lives of the children who they would eventually welcome into their home, his grounding in factory work kept Martin humble throughout all his future career successes.

Martin tells me that as a teenager leading a chaotic lifestyle, he was saved by the kindness of two families who looked out for him and provided a sanctuary away from his own unhappy home. "Twice I was saved by families who took me in when I needed it and gave me a roof over my head. Both of those families always had space for me and their care showed me that there was a different way of life to what I'd seen growing up with my own family. Even though my own upbringing wasn't perfect, my time with those two families showed me that there was another way of living, a better way of life. Looking back at those years I now realise that I experienced fostering myself, only in a very informal way".

Emigrating back to England when he turned nineteen, Martin feels he "got lucky" by meeting his future wife quite quickly and falling in with a good group of people who looked out for him. Martin began to flourish from the secure base he found in having people who valued him as a person. As well as becoming their news editor, he would go on to enjoy twenty-four years in other roles for *The Times* as part of a career in journalism that spanned more than three decades. To this day he continues to work as a freelance journalist, alongside the roles in PR and media consultancy he fits in with being a foster carer.

I've heard from several people that the Form-F process used to assess potential foster carers in England is one of the most demanding and personal assessments people can be put through. Your employers are contacted, every aspect of your past is explored and your motivations for wanting to take unknown children into your home are picked apart. Martin confirms this view of fostering assessments but, rather than dwelling on the gruelling nature of such a grilling that others have, he instead tells me how he found the process cathartic. "I used to blame myself for what happened in my childhood but exploring those feelings in my fostering assessment helped me see the truth of what I'd lived through. It made me come to the realisation that none of what had happened in my childhood was actually my fault".

Martin's realisation that none of what happened to him during his childhood was his fault had a big impact on his later life, helping him to reframe the story of his early years. Hearing the manner with which he speaks about this experience really struck a chord with me and brought back memories of many children I've worked with in the past who, just like Martin used to, blame themselves for what is going on around them. After Martin describes the positive impact that being able to address those misconceived feelings had on him, I'm left wondering just how many adults are out there in the world still carrying the burden of accountability for what they went through as children.

Shaped by his own past experiences of being taken in and cared for by families during his times of need, Martin and his wife Lorna raised their two daughters in an open household. "Our home was a bit of a sanctuary of our daughters' friends" he explains. "There was always an extra seat at the table for anybody who needed a meal and our daughters' friends would often be over talking to Lorna about their lives, feeling they could share things with her they couldn't with their own Mums and Dads". One of these conversations saw Lorna finding out that one of her daughters' friends was about to be made homeless. A few weeks later the entire family of five had moved in and ended up staying for three months until they found a new home of their own. Seeing positive outcomes like this, combined with their own childhood experiences and desire to give something back to the world, led to Martin and Lorna becoming foster carers by the time their daughters were adults.

Now, after nine years of caring for children and held in high regard as a prominent figure in the world of foster carers, I ask Martin to give me his own State of the Union address so that I might better understand just what it's like to be a foster carer in 2017. He doesn't pull any punches or sugar-coat the gritty reality of caring for children on behalf of the state.

"Local Authority cuts to fostering are unsustainable. We are short of foster carers as it is and those that we still have are getting older. The average carer is in their mid-fifties and that age is increasing over time. In five-to-ten years' time, the current system will no longer be sustainable. There's nothing on the horizon to address these issues and the care of vulnerable children is falling down the list of political priorities. In the fight for recognition, the social care challenge of an ageing population will end up being seen as more important because it's something that more people are familiar with. Most voters will have at least one elderly relative in need of care, most won't have a child in their family who has been taken into care".

Martin first shares his prediction about adult social care taking precedent with me in February 2017. Less than a month later, on the 8th of March, The Chancellor of the Exchequer, Philip Hammond, gave his Spring Budget to Parliament. His speech contained the headline grabbing announcement that councils were to receive an extra two billion pounds to fund adult social care over the following three years. There were no such concessions for children's social care. As both a current foster carer and esteemed journalist, Martin clearly has his finger on the pulse when it comes to such issues.

I put it to Martin that such moves from the Conservative government will likely appeal to the electorate as well as their own backbenchers who've been put under pressure from constituents starting to feel the bite of austerity creeping into the more affluent parts of our country. He's in full agreement that such a move is politically smart and a reaction to a winter of news headlines focussing on 'bed blocking' and 'winter pressures' faced by the NHS. As we discuss the political landscape of social work further (particularly the controversial Children and Social Work Bill that is being passed back and forth between the House of Commons and the House of Lords at that time) Martin shares his view that seeking political support is only one part of better caring for children in need. He argues that instead of simply looking towards our politicians to solve the issues we face, we need to look at changing our society and culture as a whole.

"As a society, we're scared to really tackle the issues that drive children into care in the first place. There's not enough public awareness of how vulnerable large sections of the general population have become. I hate to use this stigmatising term, but there is an 'underclass' of millions of people who have been totally marginalised in our society. We don't provide the support that marginalised people need to develop as human beings or give them a chance to break the cycles of deprivation they're living in. Children end up paying a high price because of parents who have never been taught how to raise a family or how to look after themselves. Add in drugs, alcohol and domestic violence to the mix and you end up with a largely ignored portion of our population that needs significant support".

As I have heard time and time again from people all over the social work spectrum, Martin lets me know that "early intervention is key" if we are ever going to stand a chance of addressing the deep divide in our society between the haves and the have nots. "The children who come to be looked after by us should never have had to go through what has happened to them. Every child we see has had missed opportunities in their life to make a difference and keep them at home with their Mums and Dads". He isn't afraid to let me know that some of these missed opportunities happen on the watch of my fellow social workers, but he also points out the role that wider communities have in ensuring children are kept safe too.

"Our society as a whole and our local communities need to take more of a stance in the duty of safeguarding children. Social workers can't solve all the world's problems on their own and need to rely on families, friends and neighbours of vulnerable children working with them. There is so much pressure on social workers right now that there is a conveyor belt of assessing risk within the system, driven by timescales set by either the courts of the councils. With more pressure and less early intervention services to help children, the worry is that social workers end up chipping away at what they're willing to accept for children, making compromises about what's best for the kids on their caseloads".

The notion of social workers being forced to compromise makes me bristle. As a proud social worker it's difficult to hear my profession, that is founded on the ideal of person-centred practice, be accused of making compromises. He's not lying though. In my own career and from the accounts of many fellow professionals I've spoken to from all over the world, there are times when the services that children and their families need are simply not available. I often say that most of the families we work with could do with a Mrs Doubtfire in their lives. They need somebody who can come in and offer real hands-on support in the home by helping get the kids to school on time, doing the washing up, reading bedtime stories and setting an example of how life can be. As naïve as this now makes me sound to him, I let Martin know that those are the kind of things I thought I'd be doing as a social worker when I first enrolled at university (without the dressing up as a woman of course).

Not only is there no legion of Mrs Doubtfire's out there, ready to be deployed in times of crisis to help keep families together, but the family support workers and early intervention services that may have fulfilled similar duties have been decimated by years of Local Authority budget cuts. My discussions with Martin come at a time

166

where councils all over the country are warning that they have reached breaking point. Their latest budgets, drafted in time for April and taking effect in 2018, will likely see even more closures of libraries, youth clubs and children's centres. The dedicated public servants who fill these buildings- librarians teaching children the joy of reading, youth workers steering teenagers away from a life of crime and family support workers keeping babies safe within their own homes- all facing restructure at best and redundancy at worst.

Like most us is in social care, Martin fails to understand the logic of a system that is so short-sighted it cannot see the overwhelming argument for early intervention. Putting money into community services right now will certainly cost us in the short-term, but lead to our local and national government saving many times more in decades to come. Children who may have ended up dependent on state handouts or part of the criminal justice system will instead have been supported into brighter futures. For a government so often spinning the argument of meritocracy as a reason for bringing back the grammar school system, cutting off large swathes of society seems at odds with the oft-repeated soundbites relating to every child deserving the chance to make something of their lives. It would appear that some children are more important than others, mostly depending on their postcode and capacity of the parents they were fated to be born to.

This difference in opportunity, dependent upon nothing more than the happenstance of which parents children are born to, is clearly shown to me when Martin begins to recount the tales of some of the children he has welcomed through his door. "The reality of the children we've cared for is so far removed from where it should be" he explains. "They've never had the opportunity to see how good life can be. Some children we've looked after have been astonished to hear that my daughters have jobs and have been taken aback to see me cook and iron. I've been called a 'girly boy' for taking on jobs around that house that they've been brought up to believe were only for women to do. We've had children who have had a ravenously unlimited appetite and will keep eating until they're sick. Children who will steal food and horde it in their bedrooms out of fear the cupboards will be bare when they wake up in the morning. Even the girls we've got living with us now will go to bed asking what we're going to be having for breakfast in the morning. They're still not used to a family sitting down and eating together every day before school".

It's a bleak picture that Martin paints about what the children he's looked after have gone though in their lives before coming into his care. As with everything he tells me though, it's a fair refection of modern life and the issues faced by foster carers across the world. I ask him if he was prepared for life as a foster carer and for the extent of the difficulties faced by the children he would be asked to look after. "Not really" he admits "we imagined having kids for a few months at a time and taking long breaks in between". Nine years later and the longest Martin and Lorna have gone without caring for children has been just over four weeks. "We developed more of a commitment to the children we looked after and a greater depth of emotional attachment than we thought we ever would".

The commitment and emotional attachment Martin speaks of has seen him going above and beyond to not only support the children placed with him, but to also take care of their families as well. "Lorna helped build up a mother whose children we had looked after and were being rehabilitated back into her care. She taught her how to shop for healthy food, how to cook, how to stock her fridge and cupboards, how to clean a house and how to manage her budget. When we went over to her house we found a mattress saturated in urine and a front garden full of broken glass, dirty hypodermic needles and used condoms. We spent our free time

168

putting the house right for the children to go home to and paid out of our own pocket to put a fence up in the garden".

Martin lets me know that the reason he and Lorna make such a commitment to care is because "our lives are the children". It is when he starts to talk about the difference that he sees in the children he's looked after that I see the passion behind this dedication. "The change that you see in children is quite profound and you see that your care always leaves a legacy. The first thing you notice are the physical changes. We've had children come to us with physical scars and injuries from abuse, malnourished, obese, underweight and in poor health through lack of exercise. They leave us happier, fitter, stronger, taller, more alert and full of energy. We teach them to spend time outdoors, to enjoy active play, to walk, to cook and how to eat properly".

"It's not just about money though" he tells me, cutting off any counter-argument that could be made regarding his middle-classed lifestyle making it easier for him to give children a healthier start to life. "None of those things- walking, playing, cooking properly, keeping clean and healthy- cost money. Yes, there is a cost in basic things such as a warm home, clean clothes and fresh bedding, but there are many poor people out there who care brilliantly for their children. People with money also neglect and abuse their children too. The dividing line is that your background, upbringing and circumstances either gives you the emotional capacity to keep your children safe or not".

With care applications in the family courts at an all-time high and no solution forthcoming, I ask Martin where he thinks we might find an opportunity to change things. "Too many children are growing up with having missed out on the most basic of life skills. These children then go on to have children of their own and we end up with parents who have no sense of how to look after themselves, manage money or safely care for their own young ones. This way of life then becomes the norm to their future generation. We must challenge this accepted norm by teaching people basic life skills when they are in school and we have a chance to shape their lives for the better".

Acknowledging the significant shift in priorities that such a course of teaching life skills would entail, Martin says "part of the problem is the way we set up our schools. We've lost the ability for teachers to sit down and chat to kids, to be their role models. The drive for children to pass their exams and for teachers to hit targets has taken over. We need to be giving kids the ability to speak out about what they're experiencing, to raise their aspirations and to give them the confidence to go home and say to their parents 'I want my life to be better than this'. You'll never get to the top of a league table for being the best school at personal and social education, but this is needed if we're serious about taking better care of our children".

The way Martin talks about 'our' children is interchangeable, he uses the same term whether talking about his own two birth daughters, the children placed with him down the years or every other child in the country. Such an approach to talking about children shows you everything you need to know about his own morality and commitment to young people. It also encapsulates his belief that a collective societal approach is needed to give our future generation the best chance they can have of making a better world for themselves.

"Fractured and scattered communities are an issue" he says when we go beyond his plans for education reform. "Family units are smaller, communities are falling apart and there aren't the same connections between people that there once were". Emigrating

170

back to England just in time to live through the prime years of Thatcherism, Martin doesn't need me to remind him of Margaret Thatcher's quotes from a *Women's Own* interview in 1987- "They are casting their problems at society. And, you know, there's no such thing as society. There are individual men and women and there are families". I wonder just how different things might have been thirty years later had our Prime Minister back then placed more focus on building societies and less on empowering individuals.

Martin's focus on the societal issues of isolation and oppression that drive so many children into the arms of their Local Authority are summed up with a story he tells me of a girl he once had in his care. "She was eight years old and she'd never been to a birthday party or had one of her own. She hadn't even once had a friend come back to her house for tea". That young girl, marvelling at a birthday cake of her own and jumping for joy at the prospect of having a friend from school come over for tea, tells you everything you need to know about how easy it is for children to drift towards the edges of society.

Returning to the invaluable role that foster carers play in keeping children safe from harm, I ask Martin to shoot from the hip and let me know what life is like on the ground for the fostering community. "We're like any group connected to public services in that we're feeling the impact of austerity. It means that resources are spread very thinly. Foster care doesn't happen in a vacuum either, so it means everything else happening within child protection hurts us too. A lot of experience has been lost from the child protection workforce and the legal system is under strain. This means that we've seen a decline in the quality of assessments put before the family courts and decisions being made for the wrong reasons. Foster carers getting older and leaving the system means that children are being placed with people who aren't always the best choice for them. All of this stress inevitably finds its way down to the children themselves".

In the time that Martin and Lorna have been foster carers, they've lived through some significant changes that have impacted on both his role and children's social care in general. From the Baby P effect that saw the number of children coming into care spike as a fallout from the negative press following the death of Peter Connelly, to plans to accredit children's social workers and bring in a new regulator. From the knock-on effects of the global financial crisis of 2008 that heralded the start of austerity, through to the Brexit vote that leaves the future of the whole country uncertain as we chart our way as a more independent nation. They've gone through a lot in their time looking after children and I ask Martin how he's seen foster care change over the past nine years.

"We love fostering and it's a brilliant thing to do, but in its current form it's unsustainable" he warns. "It's more difficult to recruit new carers than ever before. We know people who've dropped out of the system forever because of the increased burdens and strains that have come over the past nine years. The costs some foster carers are being asked to bear is unsustainable and it's leaving many of us out of pocket. The fostering population is getting older and there aren't any young people being attracted in to replace us. The career as we know it will soon wither and I don't think we're too far away from Local Authorities having to reconsider opening all the old children's homes again".

With Martin's experience in public relations and marketing, it doesn't come as a surprise to hear him go to town on the current failing efforts to recruit foster carers and promote the benefits of becoming one. "By focusing their advertising campaigns on the money that carers can potentially earn, Local Authorities

172

are alienating a huge section of society like me and Lorna. I think there are many foster care success stories out there that will show people the benefits of care but we've failed to tell those stories. Any success we have ends up being clouded by statistics that show children who've been in care are more likely to end up in prison. That's unfair because we need to be judged on how well children have done since coming into care, not what's happened over the course of their whole lives before we had a chance to look after them".

The point he makes about the negative image surrounding care experienced young people is a pertinent one and he's right to point out the link that is constantly made between children being in care and poor life outcomes. Lazy reporting on this issue seeks to directly connect care experience with teenage pregnancy, crime, drug use and poor engagement with education. On the surface, such figures are correct and young people who've experienced care are far more likely to be young parents (Fallon & Broadhurst, 2016) and spend time in prison (Prison Reform Trust, 2017). However most of the reporting into this area fails to acknowledge that foster care itself would likely have had little bearing on such poor outcomes, with children's lives significantly damaged by the abuse and neglect they experienced before coming into care.

Research into the stress hormone cortisol by Professor Vivette Glover (2016) has found that this hormone, when evoked in stressful situations experienced by a mother, crosses the placenta and is absorbed by her unborn child. Glover's research shows that stress caused by events such as arguing or violence from a partner causes unborn children to absorb an unnaturally high amount of cortisol. She identifies that particularly frightening scenarios, where the baby's mother is faced with needing a 'fight or flight' response, are especially damaging to unborn children. Her research showed that babies who were exposed to the highest levels of stress-related cortisol during their time in the womb had lower IQs by the time they were 18 months old. The same babies were also more likely to be anxious and fearful in their behaviours and mannerisms during later life.

This kind of research helps to challenge the false narrative that foster care is bad for children. In fact, when care experienced young people are spoken to about their time in care, many speak positively of their experience (Coram Voice, 2015). As well as this unfair and unbalanced reporting on the supposed harm of care that fails to mention the debilitating impact of what came before children were identified as being at risk, Martin feels that fostering gets a bad reputation because it is seen as being second best to the permanency of adoption. "I deeply resent the notion that fostering doesn't provide a stable and loving long-term home and that it is inferior to adoption. The Government's pro-adoption stance doesn't help and neither does our lack of a unified voice for foster carers or a champion of the good that we achieve". Martin finishes his lament about the poor regard for foster carers by adding "we're taken for granted and because of this there's a belief that we're always going to be there, that we're replaceable if we can't tough it out. Not having a unified voice or anyone championing our cause makes the issue even worse".

I don't want to put any pressure on Martin, but I must mention the glaringly obvious point that he might just be the champion of foster carers he says is so very much needed. He shies away from claiming such a title but he does respond to my probing when I ask him to tell me what such a champion would strive for. "There needs to be a unified and coherent approach to promoting the needs of foster carers. I've never seen a foster campaign that hasn't been more about promoting the organisation behind it than the good of foster care itself. There's no national campaign that seeks to promote our good work and, in doing so, attract new people into the career. We should also be moving towards professional ac-

174

creditation for carers as a recognition for the skill and expertise that goes into what we do. Instead of just focusing on meeting the most basic of needs for children coming into care, to keep them safe and give them a home, we should aspire to more. We need to be ambitious and bold for the kids who come into care and those of us who look after them".

Martin wouldn't thank me for saying it, so I don't at the time, but he certainly talks like the champion that he says foster carers need so badly. His talk of a figurehead who can drive change is something that echoes much of what I have heard from within my own professional community over the years. The counter-argument against pinning all our hopes on some sort of champion has been that it's too much pressure to put on one person and lifting up an individual to represent us all isn't a very collaborative thing to do. I'm inclined to side with Martin though and feel that every great movement in history has needed some sort of leader to band around. If I were a foster carer, I'd be glad to have him batting for my team.

It isn't just about finding a leader or starting a campaign to promote change for Martin, he believes addressing the issues he shares with me relies on more than that. "My dream is that fostering moves away from becoming a job that people do and towards a social movement. The care of children who come into care shouldn't just be a duty carried out by the Local Authority or the people paid to take them into their homes, it should be the responsibility of the whole community. For example, why not do things like approaching businesses in the area to ask if they'll allow children in care to access local services and adventure parks for free?". It sounds like a Blue Peter badge for local children in care and it also sounds like a brilliant idea.

Forward-thinking ideas like this are greatly needed but Marin admits that getting the whole community to buy into the idea of supporting looked after children is a big ask. "Foster carers work on the fringes of society. When a child is taken into care the whole community becomes suspicious and defensive. Mums and dads worry that they are going to be blamed for something. There's a feeling that foster carers are agents of the state, there to snoop on other children at school. We have to work hard to persuade other families that we need their help to make the placement work."

It's not just the view of people who know children who've gone into care and the communities that surround them that needs to change for Martin. He also shares his opinion that there are "nasty arguments" that need to be challenged. The type of arguments that see people looking down on their fellow citizens, sneeringly asking "what is the point of working with these people?" or "why should these people be having kids?" need challenging.

There's a lot that social workers can learn from Martin's experience and commitment to fostering, so I ask him what we can do to help people who are looking after children that we have taken into care. "Take us seriously. Trust our views, especially on issues such as contact and how children present before and after seeing their parents. Listen to us. It sometimes feels like we're seen as nothing more than providers of bed and breakfast for children and this devalues us. We may not be professionals but we need to be listened to and respected. At times, we can tend to get cut out of the conversations in looked after reviews and meetings when other professionals are involved. It makes carers feel really bad".

Martin gives me two examples of how poorly foster carers can feel they are treated by the social care system. The first of these involved a carer who was told by a social worker she would be taking a new-born into her care straight from hospital. She visited the baby and mother in hospital as soon as she was informed of the placement, told her family to expect a baby coming into their home soon and went out to buy everything needed to welcome their new arrival. On the day of the planned discharge she turned up at hospital to be told that the baby was now going home with her mother. Great news of course, but she found out that this decision had been made four days earlier. She was allowed to visit that hospital every one of those four days to bond with the baby and learn from her mother how she wanted her little girl looking after. Nobody from children's services thought it was worth telling the foster carer about the change of plan. As Martin says, "there was a complete disregard for the feelings of the foster carer. She was seen as a solution to a problem and when that problem no longer existed, her feelings didn't matter".

The second story he shares with me is just as sad. This time it involved a little boy who couldn't go back to his birth-parents and ended up being adopted as a toddler. He was in foster care for a fair amount of time before a family was found for him and during his period in care developed a particularly strong and loving bond with the foster carers' twelve-year-old daughter. He grew to look up to her like a big sister and she shared this bond, seeing him as the little brother she'd never had. "She dearly loved that little boy" Martin tells me. "When the adoption became final the adoptive mother came out and sad 'I don't want anything at all to do with the foster carers' because she didn't want to be reminded of her adopted son's time in care. The foster carers daughter was absolutely devastated by that news and was left heartbroken".

These feelings of being cast aside by the system when a better option presents itself aren't just felt by others, with Martin sharing a few tales of his own that reveal just how hard it can be saying goodbye to children you've nurtured for well over a year. "The system presumes that we carers should have no contact with a child for over three months after they've moved on. Apparently, it's because evidence suggests this is best for the child, but that's hard to believe. It's really unpleasant to go through that loss and one of the worst experiences you can imagine".

For all the difficulties faced by foster carers and for all the low times, Martin maintains that caring "is one of the best things you can do". He passionately tells me that "you get more out of it than you'll ever put in. The small daily victories, such as teaching a little girl how to tell the time or tie her shoelaces, make it all worthwhile". The way that he talks so lovingly and devotedly about fostering fills me with hope that there are people like him and Lorna out there ready to give a home to children in need, but also leaves me a little deflated with knowing just how unappreciated and taken for granted Martin and his fellow carers can feel. With a shrinking and ageing pool of foster carers combined with ever-increasing numbers of children going into care, I'm left agreeing with Martin that the system as it stands is unsustainable.

As we say our final goodbyes, I ask Martin to draw things to a close with a message of hope that all of us connected to children's social care can cling on to. He doesn't let me down. "Society sits at an apex right now, with the impact of Brexit meaning that so many things we took for granted are no longer assured. It leaves worry and uncertainty, but it also gives a chance to change our way of thinking. So many things are up for grabs and we can begin to rethink our priorities for the future. A radical approach is needed to care for vulnerable children, so let's start again and try to get things right for them".

After speaking with Martin over the course of a couple of weeks, we part for the last time and he goes back to his life as a father, husband, foster carer, writer and media consultant. He leaves me with a lot to think about and I start to see subtle shifts in my own work straight away. I always had a lot of respect for the foster carers I worked with because of the invaluable role they played, but I began developing an increased sense of reverence for their work. The stories Martin shared of how often carers can feel forgotten about and devalued have an especially profound effect on me. I double-down on my appreciation of the foster carers I stand shoulder-to-shoulder with and promise myself I'll never leave them feeling like the carer who spent four days bonding with a new-born who was never coming home with her or the twelve-year-old girl who felt like she'd lost her little brother.

I hope that Martin and his fellow foster carers find the change they desperately need. I hope that the movement he dreams of becomes a reality, fuelled by a political and societal momentum that says we will no longer accept a life of mediocre safety as the best we can expect for abused and neglected children. Most of all, I hope that Martin sees how he might just be the champion of foster care that he's looking for.

Chapter Fourteen: Falling in a failing Authority

I never realised how much it was getting to me until one day I was driving from a home visit to a meeting and I felt like driving head on into another car at seventy miles an hour. I saw the cars rushing past me on the other side of the road, saw the speed I was doing and saw my hands resting on the steering wheel. A slight turn to the right, a momentary movement in my muscles and it would all be over. My life snuffed out in a second and all my worries gone for good. No more being asked to justify why my visits were put on the system late, no more being threatened by angry parents who would rather deflect problems onto me than accept the part they had to play in the abuse their own children had been subjected to, no more emails where all the things I hadn't found the time to do were marked in red for the whole team to see. No more working until 3am to get court reports finished, no more having to get in the office first to claim one of the desks in a quieter space where you could hear yourself think, no more phone calls to tell my husband that I'd be late home again tonight.

Peace. Release. Oblivion.

The temptation to send myself veering across the road and into an innocent driver lasted no longer than a few seconds before I quickly gathered myself and felt ashamed that such a dark thought had found its way into my mind. I turned up the radio, took another sip of my diet coke and sped on towards the meeting I was already running late for. The temptation may have passed in a few seconds, but the memory of that feeling has stayed with me ever since. I had two sons and a step-daughter, a dear husband and a large family that meant everything to me. I had a nice house in the suburbs, took two holidays a year and my parents were proud of me. I had all the trappings of a nice life. Yet, despite everything I had to live for, I'd been tempted to end it all.

You think that depression will creep in slowly and come over you like twilight does with the setting sun. You imagine it getting worse and worse as, day by day, you gradually start to lose your lust for life. That's how it looks from the outside at least. What you don't envisage is it blindsiding you on a quiet Tuesday afternoon in late October. Katy Perry blasting out of the radio, diet coke to hand, mentally preparing your latest excuse for being late, and thoughts of causing a head on collision coming out of nowhere.

When the realisation finally hits home that you're depressed, you start to look back and piece together all the little bits that led you to this point. The best way I can think of describing it is how one day you look in the mirror and realise that you've gotten old. The grey hairs come in one by one, the wrinkles appear over time and the boobs start slowly but surely sagging. It doesn't happen over-night, but one day you end up staring back at a face that's old and it dawns on you that you're the same age your mother was when you first started going out to local nightclubs and felt that your ado-lescence would go on forever.

Just like all those grey hairs that I plucked out and forgot about as soon as they appeared, the days and weeks following that journey between appointments saw me begin to look back at all the warn-ing signs about my mental wellbeing that I'd casually dismissed. I'd put my constant grumpy moods down to getting older and as I would often joke 'turning into my mother'. I suspected that my anxiety and forgetfulness was a result of perimenopause, the transitional stage before menopause. I blamed my worry-fuelled sleepless nights on not working hard enough to keep all the plates spinning. The magazines I read were full of women who had successful careers, happy home lives, baked beautiful looking cakes and still found the time to keep in shape by going to the gym five times a week. I could do the same if I gave up some of the things that I did in my free time, like watching the soaps or reading the same trashy magazines that ultimately made me feel worse about myself.

The last thing I thought to blame was my work. Of course it was hard, that's what social work was. Of course it was stressful, every job worth doing is. Of course it created pressure, that's what drove me on to do the best I could. The difficulties I encountered weren't unique to me, everyone else in my team was under the same pressure and working under the same spotlight of management oversight. The problems weren't even unique to my team. All the places I'd worked before had the same problems of high caseloads, poor support services and the feeling that you never quite had enough hours in the day to get everything done that you wanted to. If I wasn't coping, it must be down to me not working efficiently enough or employing the right time management techniques. As a temporary manager who was once brought into our department as a trouble shooter told me, I should be working "smarter, not harder".

Carrying the burden of blame for inefficiency on my own shoulders and putting the clear discontent amongst my team down to social workers liking to moan, I carried on regardless by brushing off all the little warning signs that things weren't quite right in my life. I grew more tired, but found sleep harder to come by. My anxiety increased, but the things that used to help me wind down after a hard day at work began to lose their potency. The grumpiness got worse and I found myself snapping at my husband or telling our kids off for the slightest little things.

I'd picked up on none of these warnings at the time though and felt that they were nothing more than character traits of the person I was becoming or signs that I had lost the fight against middle-age. It was only in the aftermath of that Tuesday afternoon's car journey that I started to look inside myself and wonder how someone like me, who had everything she ever wanted out of life, could have ended up briefly wishing for it all to end. When I started to piece together the puzzle, I saw that my downfall had mirrored the deterioration of the team I had been a part of for more than three years. My falling down had mirrored the failing of the Local Authority.

When I first walked into our office I found a settled team brimming with experience and confidence. There were only two newly qualified social workers, no agency staff and our manager had been in post for eight years, having worked in the team herself before moving up the ladder. All good signs that this was somewhere I could settle down long-term and start to overpay my pension in the hope of a slightly early retirement. The first year went by without incident and then the news started to spread that we were going through a 'transformation project'. The council had to save £50 million pounds by 2020 and every service they provided was under review. The rumours spread like wildfire that we'd go the way of neighbouring authorities by losing our libraries, community hubs, youth clubs and children's centres. We had faith that we'd be alright in social work because, as a statutory service, the council had to keep us going.

Our faith paid off and we kept our jobs. That didn't bring us much happiness when everyone else that we worked alongside with was losing theirs though. The youth clubs closed, even the flagship one that they'd opened to great fanfare only four years ago. Half of the children's centres shut their doors and the ones that remained open had to lose some of the most popular groups because they could no longer afford to bring people in to run them.

184

The smaller libraries were mothballed and services were centralised in the larger ones. The money that used to prop up local community groups disappeared. Bin collections moved to fortnightly.

Although we kept our jobs, the way we did our work started to change as well. The petty cash limit dropped, there was a new finance panel introduced, every expense over a certain threshold had to be signed off by our service manager, the pot of money we kept for child in need cases was taken away. Instead of being able to put five pounds on somebody's electric card or go to the shops to buy nappies and baby food, we instead had to support people in ringing up for a crisis loan or signpost them to the nearest foodbank.

You started to get emails going around about the hundreds of thousands of pounds we were spending on printing every year. The process for claiming back your mileage expenses became more convoluted than ever. A new process was brought in where you had to re-book taxi forms for looked after children every single month, even if they'd been in placement for years and nothing at all had changed. I wasn't naïve and I knew that national austerity measures were being applied all over the country, but it felt like this extra financial scrutiny was such a terrible waste of time and left us with even fewer opportunities to see the children on our caseloads.

It wasn't long after these new ways of counting every single penny came in that we started to see children's services squeezed by increasing demand. We had more children coming into care than ever before but no money to bring in additional workers to supervise contact with their parents. The burden shifted to the social workers and I found myself spending at least two afternoons a week, plus most duty shifts, supervising contact. With most of the places we used for contact having shut their doors or now charging for room hire in an effort to stay afloat, children were spending what little time they got with their parents in stale old office rooms.

The pressure of having to do more with less, and of having to justify every aspect of your work to the accountants, became too much for some people and they started to leave. Experienced workers were replaced with newly qualified ones who, for all their intelligence and enthusiasm, weren't cut out to be taking on the caseloads they were being given. The gaps in the workforce started being filled by short-term agency workers who initially came from the local area but, when that well ran dry, started being shipped in from all over the country. As friendly as these new workers were, there was an uneasy sense of uncertainty that people perhaps weren't too committed to the area. Sometimes we would have people come in on Monday and be gone by Friday.

My manager took early retirement as part of a redundancy package and was replaced by somebody who was taking up their first managerial post. She was dedicated, committed, idealistic and genuinely tried her hardest to succeed. The job she walked into wasn't the right one to start out in as a manger though. When things got difficult her reaction was to work later and harder. It was common for me to get emails from her at 4am and then see her as the first person in the office four hours later. There was a rumour doing the rounds that her husband begged her to quit after a doctor had told them that her high levels of stress were making it hard for her to become pregnant. She was replaced by the same manager who came in with a reputation of being a trouble shooter that told me I should be working "smarter, not harder" when I mentioned the lack of time I had to do all that he wanted from me.

The caseloads crept up, the support services continued to drop

186

off, teams kept turning over, and you noticed more and more emails bouncing back from people who were on long-term sickness leave. Nobody ever admitted that sickness was so high because of stress and burnout, but it was obvious to us all. It was inevitable that standards would start to drop as a result.

Paranoid senior managers, who were frightened they'd lose their jobs if improvements weren't made, started to blame their social workers for everything that was going wrong. Their master plan to save their own skins was to bring in new procedures, templates and processes that aimed to standardise our working practices. The implication was that it was us social workers who were failing and we had to improve. Rather than bringing about the hoped-for improvements, the added pressure of additional scrutiny and accountability resulted in even more people handing in their notices of resignation.

In three years, I had gone from being the newest member of our team to the only one left from the day I walked in. Even our admin staff had changed and been replaced by a rotating pool of workers who we had to book in advance if we wanted a minute taker.

It was only when I realised that I was suffering from depression that I put everything together and saw how all the pressures of work were being internalised. In accepting that social work was changing and believing the narrative that I was to blame for not keeping up with the times, I was carrying the burden of everything that I wasn't able to achieve. Minutes from meetings weren't late because of unrealistic expectations on my workload, they were late because I wasn't typing fast enough. Reports weren't filed minutes before their deadlines because I was being set impossible targets, they were filed at the last minute because I hadn't front-loaded my assessment work. Plans weren't progressing because the services that would have helped make meaningful changes were all closing, they were drifting because I wasn't good enough at my job.

You can only beat yourself up about things and call yourself a failure for so long until something must give. What gave way for most of the people I used to work with was their job, with them giving up on the empty promises of senior managers 'turning the ship around' and walking out. What gave way for me was my happiness.

As I set my thoughts down in writing in the hope that people might learn from what I've been through, it looks as if the realisation about what my job had done to me came quickly. That's not the case though. Even after that stupid desperate thought of crashing my car, it took me many weeks to piece everything together and to see just what had become of me; to finally come to the dawning realisation that I was working myself into an early grave for £32,800 a year.

My GP diagnosed me with anxiety and depression. I was prescribed Sertraline to help with my low mood and Loprazolam to help me sleep. This was to be followed up by a course of cognitive behavioural therapy when I'd gone through the initial triage process via a telephone interview.

I was signed off from work and the latest agency manager didn't seem in the slightest bit surprised when I called in to give her the news. She'd seen so many workers burn out that, by the time my call came through, it was likely one she was very much used to. She was similarly nonplussed when my notice was handed in just before Christmas.

Social work is a job that I loved. Even in those latter days when it all became so difficult, there were still moments of pure joy when you knew you'd made a real difference. The problem is that those moments were getting few and far between, with a feeling that direct work was something you had to fit in between all the paperwork instead of something that formed the bones of your working life.

I don't want to walk away forever and I feel like I'm ready to go back into work now, but I'm not sure I could return to the kind of job that I was doing. There's too much pressure and paperwork to make the kind of difference you want to these days.

Chapter Fifteen: The truth about social work

"All great literature is about people's lives. Hate, love, anger, compassion, that's what great writing is about. We see all of those emotions in social work, so why not write about what we experience in this career?".

Matt Bee has a lot to say about life as a social worker and he's not afraid to say it. From articles about alcohol where he reveals 'I drink largely because of stress and for this I blame social work', to blogs about the magical properties of chocolate that can help social workers achieve peak performance at the same time as keeping themselves out of jail, he is something of an *enfant terrible* within the profession; a cat amongst the pigeons of a workforce whose literary heritage is dominated by functional academic writing and gritty real-life tales of tragedy.

As I've also found out to my detriment, daring to put your head above the parapet comes at a price, and Matt has experienced the backlash that comes with daring to be a disruptor of the *status quo*. Online comments on his article about social work stress driving him to having a few drinks every night before bed called for his sacking. One anonymous commenter suggested he should be sacked because having a drink made him unfit to work with vulnerable people. Another wrote 'If social workers cannot handle their jobs then get the hell out of social work now'. Another article he wrote, this time about feeling guilty for spending so much money on coffee when there are millions of starving children in the world, led to calls that he was having a go at his fellow professionals for allowing themselves a little luxury. 'I think Matt Bee oversteps the mark if he wants to stop the general public buying coffee' was one response that stuck with him.

"I really struggled with the negative feedback at first" Matt admits when sharing his experience of writing about social work whilst still in a frontline role. "I thought people would support me and the way I was writing about genuine issues faced by social workers would be welcomed with open arms. Instead I got comments like 'if you can't hack the work don't bleat on about it', suggesting that I should put up or shut up. Other critics said that I was moaning or whinging, that I should get another job. But if a social worker has the power to take a child away from their parents or detain an adult, why can't we comment on the personal toll that such things take on us? Why can't we have an honest look at how many of us are dependent on caffeine, alcohol and junk food without facing a beating from the holier than thou brigade?".

"I've had criticism from people saying I'm damaging social work for pointing out the flaws in the system. I was trying to be honest and engage people in the truth of what those of us who are still out there doing this job every single day are facing, but some people didn't like it". Matt's description of those early critics brings to mind the words of Teddy Roosevelt that were once passed my way at a time when I was feeling particularly low in the face of mean-spirited criticism:

It is not the critic who counts; not the man who points out how the strong man stumbles, or where the doer of deeds could have done them better. The credit belongs to the man who is actually in the arena, whose face is marred by dust and sweat and blood; who strives valiantly; who errs, who comes short again and again, because there is no effort without error and shortcoming; but who does actually strive to do the deeds; who knows great enthusiasms, the great devotions; who spends himself in a worthy cause;

192

who at the best knows in the end the triumph of high achievement, and who at the worst, if he fails, at least fails while daring greatly, so that his place shall never be with those cold and timid souls who neither know victory nor defeat.

The Man in the Arena- Theodore Roosevelt

After sixteen years of writing (his first published piece coming in *The Telegraph* when he won a young journalist's award for writing about his other passion in life, cars, back in 2001) Matt has learned to give himself more credit for his efforts and to take pride in putting himself out there in the arena. "People need to know it's okay to admit that we're human in social work" he explains to me when speaking about how he managed to break through the negative criticism from his peers and keep writing. "Most people writing about social work are always trying to escalate the issues we face and link our problems to political ideologies. There's a place for such writing, but focusing on theoretical issues alone means that we miss hearing about the basic reality of day-to-day social work. Most social workers aren't thinking about neoliberalism, they're worrying about answering the phone, making sure their visits are recorded and getting home in time to see their kids before bed".

"This over-focus on politics and research in most social work writing moves us away from the human issues that most of us are facing. It makes our profession look like nothing more than a political football that is at the mercy of whatever MP decides we're worth taking an interest in. We are not powerless. We need to stop portraying ourselves as victims and start talking more about what we do and what it's like to do it. That new portrayal has to start from the ground up and it has to start by hearing more from the people who are out there doing this work, not the people who are watching us do it".

Matt's point about observers offering criticism from the side-lines reminds me of arguments I've heard from others who have pointed out that there are too many people watching social workers and not enough doing the job itself. As well as often hearing this backlash against the scrutiny that is rife in modern social work, I've also experienced at first-hand the impact that being under the spotlight can have on my fellow professionals. I've seen whole teams crumble under the pressure of an Ofsted inspection. I've been approached by a social worker who feared her colleagues would be driven to suicide by the burden of consultants scrutinising every aspect of their work. I've known many workers hounded out of the career for good because of performance management techniques that reduce the output of their efforts to nothing more than digits on a spreadsheet. It is the experiences of people like this that Matt wants to give voice to with his writing.

"If you can write about the issues we experience and highlight the problems we face then you stand a chance of getting people to listen to what we've got to say" he explains. "If you get people to listen then you get people to think. If you get people to think then you get people to change their perception of social workers. When I was 'just' a social worker saying these things in my office and with my friends nobody would listen to me. I'd go along to a meeting, share my views, someone taking minutes would politely nod their head then write my words down on paper. Those minutes would get typed up, filed away and forgotten about. But if we can get our views out to the public instead of sharing them in tokenistic team meetings or focus groups, people will pay attention".

Matt goes on to give me the example of how quickly Local Authorities react when a negative news story about a failed inspection or serious case review hits the local press. The reactions to this kind of public pressure- promises that lessons will be learned, making extra funding available and bringing in new workers- shows the changes that drawing attention to our struggles can bring about. He certainly makes a compelling argument for social workers engaging with traditional and social media, one that I fully agree with, but he also offers the disclaimer that speaking out as a social worker can come at a cost.

"After submitting my first article about social work I remember hearing the news it was going to be published and telling my manager. Her reaction wasn't to share in my joy or congratulate me. Instead she looked at me with a poker face and said she'd have to speak to our service manager about it. Two days later I had an email forbidding me from writing any further articles and informing me that I'd broken protocol by writing about my job. I looked everywhere in my contract and in our council guidance for the protocol I'd supposedly broken and couldn't find a thing apart from what I'd known already, that I couldn't mention the council's name in any written work without their approval, which I'd been careful not to. But it turned out this wasn't enough. The issue was escalated to a vice director who insisted on seeing everything I wanted to submit to magazines in advance, even though I wouldn't mention the council. That censorship of my writing came with the caveat that I wasn't allowed to put anything forward that could be seen as controversial or critical of my employer".

Matt handed his notice in within a week of being given this ultimatum about his writing and left his job two months later.

"It made me realise that I didn't really want to work for them anymore. The double standard was shocking. I'd spent years trying to get managers to listen to the concerns of those of us working on the frontline with vulnerable adults and getting nowhere. Yet as soon as I said that my writing was good enough to be published by a national social work magazine I had a hotline straight to the

195

vice director. The article that got me into trouble was about having to wait nine hours for an ambulance to take an elderly service user to hospital. As this was a Mental Health Act assessment there was no choice but to wait, and as we had been called out late in the day we had to work almost 24 hours straight by the time we clocked off. At work the next day I explained to my manager how unsafe I'd felt and tried to raise the issue of workers who were being put in such a position. Very little changed. But when I wanted to share what I'd been through, a long wait for an ambulance, as a way of highlighting cutbacks in public services, I got into bother for fear that it would make my employer and the ambulance service look bad".

For every person like him who is brave enough to defy the will of their employer, Matt believes there are thousands more who would love to speak out about what they're seeing but are scared into submission. With the threat of HCPC sanctions and a negative reference hanging over them, combined with the need to keep a roof over their heads and food on the table, Matt doesn't blame anyone who fears that openly sharing their opinions will cost them their livelihood. He believes that this culture of fear is one of the main reasons why the narrative of social work is dominated by those who aren't doing the job and people who are in privileged positions where they can speak out without fear of recrimination.

"If a social worker comes out and says 'this place is a shambles', their employer won't support them to fix the issues they're highlighting but will instead worry that they're going to become a target. It comes down to a blame culture of people being terrified that they might be held accountable for a failure in the system. If you look at what happened to Haringey after the Baby P story came out, you can see that the entire nation's media was attracted to them. Seeing what happened there, it's no wonder other Local Authorities are scared of the truth getting out. I wasn't happy with my director acting like he did in trying to censor me, but I did appreciate why he felt he had to take such a stance. Going on like this forever, by keeping our heads down and trying to avoid attention, will get us nowhere and we need to start telling people what social workers really do in their communities".

I've heard this call for spreading the news by standing up for social work many times before but, as Matt points out, such movements have struggled to gain momentum because most social workers have been tethered by fear of speaking the truth. With pressure from employers, critics and people with a grievance against social workers combined, it doesn't surprise me that most people fear to tread the path that Matt has taken. Indeed, it is such a solitary path that, at the time I'm getting to know Matt, he is the only practising social worker in the country regularly writing under his own name. It is a fact that shames me because, even though I blog about social work every evening and millions of people see my work online every week, I don't have the courage to put my name out there like Matt does.

"Doctors and nurses help people. Teachers help people. The police catch bad guys. This is the image that people have of other professions but when people think of social workers it's either about us making mistakes or stealing children. We are painted as pantomime villains in television soaps and as demons in the national press. The only way to change this negative image is to come out of the shadows and start telling people what we really do. A lot of this change can start with the power of writing". Matt's passion for telling the truth about social work shines through and his argument for the power of the written word is a compelling one, so I'm interested in asking him what advice he has for people who want to start writing about their professional experiences.

"Keep a journal to begin with and write down whatever you're feeling, make sure you enjoy it though. Ideas are precious so, for a while at least, keep what you're writing to yourself. Critics kill writing which means if you start developing your craft in the public domain you risk being suffocated by negativity before you've even had a chance to spread your wings. Don't try to be too clever or think that you have to back up everything you're saying with facts and figures that support your way of looking at things either. It's okay to just share your feelings and offer your views. Write what you feel in your heart, not what you think will impress people. Good writing that engages people looks nothing like your best assignments from uni".

"When you've got some thoughts down on paper that you think might make a good piece of writing, you can begin trying to refine it. Always start with the passion first and then the refinement later. If you want to engage with people, you need to have writing that is going to grab people's attention and that comes from being passionate about what you're saying, not from firing out a list of facts and figures like you're in a lecture hall again. Social workers don't want to come home from a hard day's work to sit and read a boring piece of writing, they want something that is going to intrigue them and grab their attention".

"Once you've got a refined piece of writing that you think people will be interested in, put it out there. You can set up a blog of your own for free or send if over to someone else to consider publishing. You won't get rich from it, but people will pay for good quality pieces and places like *The Guardian* are always on the lookout for new writers. Prepare yourself for critical feedback but try to do what I've done by learning to embrace those negative comments. It means that you're ruffling a few feathers and that's a good thing!".

His advice is sound and I can only hope that more people follow his lead by being brave enough to share their views about social work with the world. We've been slow to grasp the power of the internet in social work and, because of this, our online engagement and social media activity lags far behind our multi-agency colleagues and most of our official websites lack inspiration. With the internet giving everybody the opportunity to engage with the masses, regardless of privilege or status, there has never been a better time for telling your own story. Matt's happy to do his bit, but he knows he's only one man and he needs more people to join him in telling the truth about social work.

What Matt says during our last hour together hits me hard and, in one short sentence, he sums up much of what is wrong with our profession right now. "Modern social work is a mixture of anger and apathy. We can't keep trying to fix things by either getting angry about the problems we face or by giving up caring. We can't keep doing the same old thing because it's getting us nowhere. We angrily blame the Government, we angrily blame the press. But what are we doing ourselves to try and change things? The best solutions I've been offered when trying to raise the profile of our issues before has been a suggestion that someone arrange a focus group. What is fifteen people sitting in a room and having a chat going to do? What difference will a hundred-people in the same old clique sharing a hashtag on Twitter make in the world?".

"As social workers, we have a responsibility to challenge where we see injustice and to do our job to the best of our abilities. If we're tied up with paperwork to the point where we can't help the people we're supposed to then that's malpractice. We have a duty to stand up and say that this way of working is wrong. The problem in raising these issues is that many social workers will be secretly angry but openly apathetic. They'll say one thing in private, or behind the guise of online anonymity, but won't dare speak out in public. I understand why, because there is so much pressure to toe the party line and keep acting in outdated ways, but if we want to go a different way we need to stand up to the fear of bullying for speaking our minds".

Matt knows not everyone has the option to walk out of a job because they're being suppressed and, had he been a parent, he might not have been able to up and leave like he did. Therein lies the reason why most social workers choose private anger and public apathy over standing up and being counted. There is simply too much at stake when paying your mortgage and looking after your children depends on keeping your job. Easier to bow down and become another cog in the machine than be seen as a troublemaker intent on going against the grain.

"Hate, love, anger, compassion", the emotions that Matt believes make social work such an interesting subject to write about all come out in our time together. He hates the way that things are going with our profession, yet he loves the people he supports and the colleagues he works alongside. He feels such anger at the disconnect between those watching social workers and those doing the job itself, but he has compassion for people who are stuck in toxic environments where they've become nothing more than timid white-collar wage slaves.

Towards the end of our time together, Matt shares a final tale with me about a man he once supported who was homeless and a chronic alcoholic. "We were talking about the risks he faced sleeping rough, his deteriorating health, and how he felt about dying. Reflecting on the prospect of sending himself to an early grave through drink, he told me 'I've got no problem with dying… it's living that I've got a problem with'. Quotes like that tell you everything about a person, what they've been through, and why telling their story and the stories of those of us who support them are so important. I want to write about social work so people get to hear our voices but, more importantly, those of people like him that we work with".

One day Matt dreams of writing a novel about social workers and getting it into the kind of households that base their view of our profession on what they read in the *Daily Mail*. If this was one of Matt's stories, now would be the point where I tell you that we parted ways with him heading off into the sunset to live happily ever after. Instead, we part ways with him heading back to life as an adult's social worker who works by day and writes by night. If he ends up failing in his quest to get more people writing about social work and to write a novel that makes it into the homes of middle England, at least he will fail greatly. He won't be like those cold and timid critical souls who neither know victory nor defeat.

Chapter Sixteen: The privilege of being a social worker

Being a social worker means…

You will never be bored.

You will always be frustrated.

You will always be surrounded by challenges, so much to do and so little time.

You will carry immense responsibility and very little authority.

You will step into people's lives and you will make a difference.

Some will bless you.

Some will curse you.

You will see people at their worst and their best.

You will never cease to be amazed at people's capacity for love, courage and endurance.

You will see life begin and end.

You will experience resounding triumphs and devastating failures.

You will cry a lot.

You will laugh a lot.

You will know what it is to be human and to be humane.

That poem is floating around all over the internet and you've probably seen it a few times yourself. Every six months or so I'll notice it going viral on social media as a new wave of people come across this anonymous musing on social work that has struck a chord with many people. Yet for all its popularity across our profession, everyone I speak to picks up on something a little different. People will view the 'difference' they have made depending upon the outcomes they have managed to achieve in their own work. Some will assume personal responsibility for 'failures' being their own fault, whereas others brush off their failings with a confidence that they did all they could to avert disaster. I'm no different and also see the content of this poem through the lens of my own professional journey in social work with adults.

The line that really sticks out for me is the finale of 'you will know what it is to be human and to be humane'. There's something about it that rings so true with all the most powerful things I've felt during my time as a social worker and how I've grown, not only as a professional, but as a man.

Like the anonymous author of this poem, I too have seen life beginning and ending. I've supported people in hospital when their own children or those of their relatives have been born. I've had to help identify the bodies of people who've had nobody else in the lives apart from ones like me who are paid to be there. Some have seen my presence during these life and death moments as an overseer of the state, tasked with intervening at times of supposed need before scuttling back to my office to record all that I have seen on clandestine computer systems. Thankfully, far more have seen my company as supportive, with some going so far as to treat me like a genuine friend. Although my professional status means I must address issues where people become overly familiar or refer to me as a friend, it's a nice feeling to know that I'm occasionally thought of in this way.

I've been blessed and I've been cursed. In the case of the blessing, the wide range of cultures and faiths I've come across has seen me receive blessings from every religious deity you can think of. I've seen people going wild during the Jewish festival of Purim and eaten the most wonderful food you've ever come across during Eid. At Christmas time, I spend my last working day before the holidays like a low-rent father Christmas, handing out gifts donated to the Salvation Army from the back of my Honda. The curses aren't quite as jolly, however they almost always come from a sense of frustration. I've learned never to take it personally and that you can always work past anger to find the true reasons for people letting loose on you. Most of the time it's about basic human needs to be loved, respected and valued not being met. Showing people how you care and that you'll help work towards a solution soon brings an end to the cursing.

Boredom is something I've never felt at work. I've been happy, sad, lonely, up, down, angry, pissed off, upset, deflated, joyous and everything else in between. I've never been bored. How can you be bored when you never know what's going to happen in the next ten minutes, let alone the next ten days?

For all the affinity that I feel with this poem, I keep coming back to the line it leaves us hanging with at the end: 'you will know what it is to be human and to be humane'. I'm invited along to a nearby university every year to give a speech as part of a first-year introduction to social work with adults. As well as putting in a few of my passions and pet peeves in an effort to play a small role in shaping our next generation of practitioners, I dwell on the importance of being humane in our social work. I'm long enough in the tooth to see the gap between the idealistic world of social work that students are trained to operate in by their degrees and the real world they will face when they take up their first jobs. The systematic workplace issues they'll have to contend with can make even the most altruistic and compassionate graduate become cynical and jaded. That's why I go along every year and tell our bright-eyed and bushy-tailed new students that they must always remember the people they are working with are just that, people.

Not clients. Not service users. Nor cases or customers. They are people, just like me and you. There but for the grace of God go I. There but for the grace of God go all of us.

A slight change in our genetics, an extra chromosome in our cells or our mother's drinking during their pregnancy. These things can shape our whole lives and result in us becoming 'service users' before we're even born. Sexual abuse at the hands of family members, being exposed to domestic violence in the home, chemical imbalances coming about with our developing brains. These factors can see us ending up as 'clients' because of what happens to us during our childhood. Being introduced to drugs by our peers, coercion into sex work by people we are in love with, an accident on the daily commute to work we've done a thousand times before. These issues can end up with us becoming a 'case'.

I've worked with rich people, poor people, the working class, middle class and upper class. I've worked with celebrities whose names you'll all have heard of and people who've got no official identity at all. Everyone is unique and all their circumstances are different. The only thing that unites every single person I've worked with is that they are, as I said earlier, simply people just like you and me. This time next week it could be you being visited by a social worker and having your quality of life in the hands of someone you've never met before. I guarantee that you won't feel like a case or a client and you certainly won't feel like a customer. It'll also be difficult for you to see yourself as a user of a service that you're not getting or might not even want in the first place. No, you'll feel like the same old person you've always been, just with a slightly different set of circumstances. You'll still like the same things, want the same things and dream of the same things, just that there might be a few extra hurdles in the way.

Seeing the human behind those hurdles is the key to being a good social worker, in my opinion at least. The people we work with are more than a set of problems that need to be solved and more than a list of issues to fix as part of our job. Just like me and you, they still think about their first kiss and the lover from that long hot summer, the one that got away. When nobody's looking they fart at will, pick their noses and wee with the toilet door open. They regret not making more of an effort to keep in touch with old friends, dream of winning the lottery and still get a little bit scared when they hear a bump in the night. Not cases, not clients, not service users. Just people.

Once you start to see your 'cases' as people, you find that your attitude towards work and resultant satisfaction in what you do begins to change. You no longer have fifty clients, you have fifty people to help. You're not closing a case, you're ending your professional relationship with a person. It's not somebody who is using the service you're providing, it's a person you're working in partnership with to help get the same basic things out of their life as everybody else is. When you start to see your work from this different angle, it begins to dawn on you how much of a gift it is to be a social worker. That's when you realise that being a social worker, and having access to the intimate lives of other people, is truly a privilege.

Chapter Seventeen: Making changes, not righting wrongs

"If you're going to come into this line of work you've got to be in it for the right reasons and the right reasons are to make a difference for the children and young people you see and you work with. Rather than looking to right any wrongs, you must look to make changes".

Jonny said those words during an interview ten months before I first spoke to him. I read the interview at the time and remind Jonny of his words during our first conversation. In his job as a social worker in one of North Yorkshire's child protection teams and his role as trustee for a National Voice (a charity run by people who have experienced care that aims to help change the system for the better), he continues to live by the ethos that coming into social work to make up for the ills of your own past is a road to ruin. Far better to make the world a better place for the people you encounter than to try and exorcise the demons from your own past.

It's now more than a decade since Jonny helped launch a National Voice and the more mature man who shares his life's story with me is very different to the young one who set out to change the care system for the better all those years ago. He's got a long-term partner, has children of his own, works part-time as a guest lecturer and is a member of a fostering panel. He's also a successful social worker who, at the time I get to hear his story, is thinking about going for his first managerial post.

He had to come through tragedy to reach these triumphs and, as I sit down to hear his story, he tells me how it all began when he was a child growing up in Bradford.

"I first started to realise things were different for me growing up when I was about seven or eight years old and had to get two buses to school by myself. My family life was difficult and filled with a lot of unhappiness for me and my sibling. None of my friends were having to do what I was and it made me think that my life wasn't the same as other people around me. I decided that I wasn't going to put up with it any longer, so I took myself off to my Aunt and Uncle's house and told them 'I'm not going home'. They couldn't look after me for too long but they did arrange for me to go and live with my Aunt's brother, Jimmy, and his wife Alison instead. It was while living with them that I started to see nicer things in life. When you're younger you don't quite understand that how you're living isn't fair until you start to see what life's like in other homes".

The point Jonny makes about feelings of normalcy regarding his own childhood is something that has stuck with him throughout the rest of his childhood and subsequent career as a social worker. With childhood poverty increasing for the third year in a row (Department for Work and Pensions, 2017) and the mass closures of early intervention services across the country, Jonny fears that the opportunity for children to glimpse another way of living is slipping out of reach. Many young people are now seeing the kind of neglect he experienced as normal because their communities are beset by poverty. Add in the lack of engagement from family support services and youth workers, who might have been able to help young people see that things aren't right at home, and you have the perfect storm of neglect compounded by abject poverty.

Experiences like that have helped shape Jonny's career as a child-centred practitioner and continue to drive on his advocacy work for young people going through the same issues he once faced. His current work is also shaped by what he saw from social workers growing up. Some of this practice was exemplary but some of it, as he recounts his first memories of engaging with a social worker, left him with a lot to be desired.

"I'd been living with Jimmy and Alison for about a year when Hugo came to see me. Apparently he was my social worker and needed to speak to me about something important. I remember him sitting down with me and suddenly hitting me with words like 'adoption', 'court' and 'judges'. I was a bold little boy so maybe he thought that being straight up with me was the best way to go. It wasn't and, although I hid it from him at the time, I was absolutely petrified by what he was telling me. I thought I was going to have to go to court like the criminals I'd seen on television. The way he spoke about wanting Jimmy and Alison to adopt me sounded so serious and I worried so much about what the rest of the family would think".

"He gave me some time to mull over what he'd been talking about and came back a week or so later. I was still so worried that I told him I didn't want to be adopted. Deep down I kind of did, but I was so scared about going to court that I would have said anything to avoid that process. Instead of working through these feelings with me and trying to understand my apprehension, Hugo decided to come out and bluntly explain the dilemma I was facing. I was told that I had the option of either being adopted by Jimmy and Alison or being sent back to my mum".

Being asked to make a crucial decision, one that stood to shape the rest of his life, in such a blunt manner is something that has stayed with Jonny forever. "So much of my work as a social worker is based on what happened in those two meetings with Hugo" he explains when reflecting on life as a nine-year-old boy faced with making a life changing decision. "He wasn't particularly bad at what he was doing or incompetent in his job, but the way he spoke about adoption terrified me into avoiding it at all costs. I was perfectly happy with Jimmy and Alison, but the planned adoption that I would have loved broke down out of my fear of processes and procedures. When I'm working with children these days I always make sure that I pitch the conversations at levels they will understand and make the discussion about their feelings, not the legal proceedings I have to undertake. When I've done my best to protect them from the cold reality of the courtroom, I ask them to repeat back to me what we've talked about to make sure they understand. That didn't happen to me and I was back living with my Mum a few weeks later".

As a profession, we can often be guilty of looking at our past through rose-tinted spectacles and yearning for the halcyon days of yore where we imagined social work was so much better than it is today. Lower caseloads, no computer systems, admin support, plentiful community services and settled teams; such working environments sound like paradise in today's world. Jonny's story of being on the receiving end of social work in the early nineties shows that we need to be a little more nuanced when romanticising the good old days. Yes, there are many facets of the profession we would welcome back with open arms, but there are also issues we should celebrate having left behind. These days we would baulk at the notion of a child having met the threshold for adoption being asked to decide whether they wanted to go through with it or go back to their parent who had neglected them, and rightly so. Jonny's story is a reminder that increased regulation of social workers, tighter legal frameworks and better managerial oversight may be stressful, but they can help improve the quality of our work with children.

Returning to the life he'd always known with his mum, Jonny moved back to his family home and life ticked over for the next four years. His case closed to children's services and slowly but surely, without professional oversight, things once again got too hard to bear at home. With the option of going to family members off the cards because he was still haunted by past fears of legal-ese, he turned to sleeping rough and sofa-surfing. The coldest and loneliest of these dark times came on nights where he ended up having to sleep in church doorways, the last one out on the streets after all his friends had gone home. "My friends' parents must have known something wasn't right" he tells me, "but nobody let social services know because people feared being seen as a 'grass' for reporting someone to the 'SS'".

"Then one day in school I got taken out of class and told that a social worker had come to see me. Right there and then I was told that I was going to become 'looked after', a label given to me that I've held onto ever since. I was told it was going to be a one-night placement with two emergency carers called Trevor and Odette. They weren't approved to take on a teenager so I was only going there until they found me another placement. I ended up staying there until I was nineteen. My children now call them 'Nanny and Grandad', I still see them every week and we go on holidays to-gether as one big family".

Within the space of four short years, Jonny's life had been shaped this way and that by his interaction with two strangers who came into his life and called themselves his social workers. I asked him how it felt to have such significant decisions made on his behalf by social workers given the power to act in his best interests. "I look back pragmatically now" he tells me, with a warmth in his voice that appears at odds with what he's spent the past few hours telling me. "I've got a wonderful partner who I love with all my heart, I'm a father to amazing children and I do a job that I adore. I'm glad that those things in my past led me to where I am now. How can I look back in anger when I've made it here? Everything I went through made me a better person and a better social worker. It taught me that, for social workers, it's just a job, but for the people we support it's their actual life".

His time living with Trevor and Odette taught Jonny the power of determination and the need to fight for causes you believe in. The first victory for his strong will came when he was allowed to stay living with Trevor and Odette for a few days longer than the one-night emergency placement it was supposed to be. Then a few weeks more and then a few months more. "I kept telling my social worker that I was quite happy there and wanted to stay. Whenever she'd talk about looking for a different placement I'd keep saying the same thing, that I wanted to stay where I was happy".

In the end, it was six years later when he finally left to get a place of his own. He shared with me his feelings at the time that "it was relief more than happiness when I found out that I could stay there for as long as I needed to. I thought 'thank God this ordeal is finally over and thank God that these people actually want me to be here'". That was a special day for Jonny and showed him the importance of standing up for what you believe in, something that he continues to do on behalf of other young people through his advocacy work with a National Voice. That was one victory chalked up for Jonny versus the arbitrary rules of his Local Authority. The next big win came on behalf of his younger sibling.

"Once I was out of the family home, the abuse turned to my sibling. They became looked after a year after me but, because Trevor and Odette didn't have a spare bedroom, they had to go to another set of carers. My sibling wasn't settled there and when we'd spend time together they'd always get upset about having to leave me to go back to their placement. I used to ask why they couldn't come and live with me and would get told it was because of a policy in place that stated each child in care had to have their own separate bedroom. It made no sense to me because we'd always shared a bedroom when we'd lived in the family home. Rules like that made me so cross at the time and even today I still see similar rules about young people in foster care that make them feel different".

There have been many improvements in the care system over the twenty years since Jonny first became involved in it and he's grateful for the progress that's been made. However, he's also seen some aspects of foster care stay the same and some of his biggest gripes remain centred on the blanket rules that young people continue to be subjected to. "Risk assessments, looked after plans and foster care standards help ensure children receive the same level of safe care, but often at the expense of letting them have a normal childhood. We try too hard to wrap kids up in cotton wool and prevent them from the things that all their friends are getting up to. If any other teenager stays out late, has a drink or smokes a bit of cannabis we say it's typical risk-taking behaviour. If a young person in care does the same thing we have to have interventions, change their care plan and put them on courses". Jonny sure talks passionately about young people in the care system and wanting their lives to be as normal as possible. He also talks a lot of sense.

With his sibling remaining in a separate placement and both still pining to live together, yet held apart by apparently unbreakable rules, Jonny was invited to his local County Hall as part of an event to show young people the workings of their children's services department. "The day ended with us all being put in a room with a man who wanted to hear about how our lives had changed since going into care. I seized my moment and went to town on everything I thought was wrong about the looked after system, especially the stupid rule which meant my sibling couldn't come and live with me. This man from the council looked a bit shocked at the time that a fifteen-year-old boy was having such a go at him and didn't really say anything back to me. After I'd ran out of steam we were all ushered out of the room and I thought I'd never be invited back again".

"When I look back on my life, I know I've made mistakes, and as a little boy lots of bad things happened to me. Parts of my life were truly awful. But would I change those terrible things if it meant giving up what I have now? Absolutely not. I see resentment and bitterness as being wasted emotions. But those pivotal moments in my life, where special people made all the difference, could have gone either way. What if Hugo hadn't scared me with his talk about court? What if Trevor and Odette didn't have a spare room that night? What if I wasn't put in a room that day and asked about my life in care?".

By the time Jonny got home from his day at County Hall, his sibling was there waiting for him in the front room with Trevor and Odette. The man Jonny had been put before was called Paul Davies and he was North Yorkshire's assistant Director of Children's Social Care. After hearing Jonny passionately deride the archaic rules that were keeping siblings apart, he "made the calls" he needed to and gave permission for them both to live with Odette and Trevor.

Reflecting on the impact that people paid to work for councils can have on the lives of children living in their areas, Jonny goes on to talk very fondly of a man he still holds in the highest esteem, the manager of his Leaving Care team, Howard Smith. "Howard always put children first" he tells me. "The needs of the care leavers he was responsible for came above and beyond anything else. Everything you need to know about what a great guy he was can be summed up by what he did one cold Autumn morning. He came into the leaving care team office (by that time Jonny was working there) and said to each of the workers 'your job today is to go out and buy every care leaver a new coat because it's going to be a cold winter'. Non-essential meetings were rearranged, report deadlines were extended by a day and every personal advisor in the room prioritised taking the young people on their caseloads out to buy a new winter coat. That was the kind of thing Howard did for children".

A man you've never met before who hears your passionate story about how unfair council rules have kept you and your sibling apart for a year, then cancels everything to prioritise your reunification that very day. Another man who cares deeply about all those he is ultimately responsible for, ensuring that care leavers get taken to the shops by their personal advisors to pick out a fresh winter coat of their choice because he cares so much about young people that he can join the dots between "it's going to be a cold winter" and "what can I do to help?". Those kinds of things stick with you for the rest of your life and it's the reason why Jonny will always hold Paul and Howard on a pedestal for all that they have done for children.

"When I started working for the council myself, the first thing I did when I got onto a computer was look up Paul Davies' details on the internal email address book. I sent him an email that same day thanking him for all that he had done for me, for going out of his way to make sure two siblings could grow up together in a home they both loved. I got a response thanking me for my kind words and welcoming me to the council. I was glad to have had the opportunity to thank him for all he'd done for me and thought that was the end of it. Years later I had the pleasure of being invited along to his retirement party. As he got up to give his farewell speech I saw him pull a piece of paper out of his pocket and, like everyone else in the room, thought it was the script for his speech"

"Instead he held the paper in his hand and began his speech without once glancing downwards at his prompt. Towards the end of the speech he began talking about the fruits of his labour and the memories of work that he would take into retirement with him. 'This' he said, unfolding the piece of paper and holding it up for those in attendance 'is the single most important email I've ever received and it shows you why we all do what we do for the children who live alongside us in our county'". It was Jonny's email thanking him for being brave enough to make a difference when an angry teenager came into his room one afternoon and started having a go at him about council rules that kept him apart from his sibling. Where most people in Paul's position might have brushed off that angry tirade and hid behind the tired old mantra of 'those are the rules' or 'that's the way we've always done things', he saw an opportunity to make a difference and took it. He read out Jonny's email to the room and nobody was left with any doubt about the rewards of putting children first.

Jonny and his sibling thrived in the care of Trevor and Odette. There's sometimes this fallacy put out that children only do well in foster care because their new carers have the financial means to provide more than their birth-parents could. The argument goes that, propped up with Local Authority funding and given the financial freedom to commit more time to raising children, foster care is a false environment that many birth-parents have no chance

218

of replicating. This unfair playing field then ends up with parents fighting a losing battle when being subject to parenting assessments and care proceedings. Jonny rejects this argument by explaining how the most important things Trevor and Odette did for him cost either very little or nothing at all. "They gave us the stable and secure home life that we'd never had before. We knew our clothes would always be clean, our beds would be made and that we'd be having tea at the same time every night. They promised that they would never hit us or hurt us. They let us know that we would always have a place to sleep. They gave us clear boundaries and set examples of how we should live".

As he recalls the sanctuary of foster care, Jonny doesn't mention pocket money, presents, holidays, fancy clothes, computer games or family cars. Instead he talks about no longer having to sleep in church doorways for fear of what might happen at home. For all the praise he gives his foster carers, he has less fond memories of the social workers who came in and out of his life at the time. "I remember many afternoons after school when I had to miss going out with my friends because my social workers were coming out to see me. They were always late and it felt like I was being grounded and punished because I was in care. Things like that were a reminder that I was different from my friends. I wanted to be a normal teenager like everyone else I was hanging around with, but social workers and their rules were setting me apart. There were times when I was told that I wasn't allowed to sleep over at my friends' homes because they hadn't been checked out. I've taken those lessons with me into my job and that need for normality is something that's always at the back of my mind".

Social work in those mid-teenage years felt like something being done to Jonny, rather than a system he was part of. This feeling that he was a bystander to the professional processes that shaped his own life was never more apparent than at times when meetings and reviews would be held about him behind his back. During one of these meetings that he wasn't invited along to, discussions were being held about his education. With his sibling now living with him and his foster placement ratified as long-term, the topic of him moving to a new school closer to Trevor and Odette's house was brought up during his latest review. The standard argument coming from social workers was that he should move to a local school to support his connection with the area that would be his home for the next five years. It was unfair to keep sending him in taxis to school every day and it was also costing the Local Authority a lot of money to keep this transport in place. Although we would have hoped to have moved on from this in the years since Jonny was at school, he tells me how the Children's Commissioner has recently published figures showing that children in care are three times more likely than their peers to be moved school in the middle of the academic year (Children's Commissioner, 2017).

"Throughout all the tough times I went through, my friends and teachers at school were the only constant that I had in my life" he tells me. "No matter what was happening at home, my friends were always there for me and often offered me a sofa to sleep on and a place of safety when I needed it most". The fact that his education was being debated by adults in a room where his view wasn't even considered still shocks Jonny to this day. Thankfully he had a champion fighting for his corner in there, his teacher Mr Ward. "Mr Ward advocated for me and wouldn't back down from his view that I was settled in school and wanted to stay there. He kept pushing the need to maintain the only constant I'd ever had in life and the importance of letting me stay where all my friends were. He was so determined that everyone else caved in and agreed that I should stay where I was happy. The council had to fund two taxis a day for years. It must have cost them a fortune, but it was so important for me".

Years later, Jonny was putting together a local awards evening for people who worked with looked after children. One of the most prestigious accolades was the 'making a difference' award whose nominees were all people who had, as the title suggests, made a difference to the lives of young people in care. Mr Ward was nominated for his dedication to looked after children in his school and won the award in its inaugural year. As chance would have it, Jonny was down to present that award and got to hand it over to the former teacher whose dedication had seem him allowed to stay at school with all his friends. The awards are still running to this day and Jonny lets me into a secret that, behind the scenes, they've given the 'making a difference' award the snappy title of "The Mr Ward Award".

Trevor and Odette, Paul Davies, Howard Smith, Mr Ward. As Jonny tells me his story of the chance encounters with people who have shaped his life, his earlier assertion that he wouldn't change one minute of his younger days becomes clearer. He has seen some of the worst of human nature from those who, by the words on the paper of his birth certificate at least, should have loved him unconditionally. Yet at the same time he has seen the best that this world can offer from people who came into his life through the lucky circumstances of choosing to pursue a life of caring for, teaching and serving the most vulnerable children in their communities.

The relationships that shaped his childhood remain dear to Jonny and, as with much of what he tells me about his own time in care, continue to shape the way he operates as a social worker. "You need to build relationships with the children and families you're working with" he tells me as he pulls out from our trip down memory lane and back into how such experiences have shaped him in the here and now. "The best social work is done on a settee, not at a desk. There's a paradox between what people tell you and what they are really thinking. The only way of breaking through that natural resistance to share secrets with a stranger is to spend time with people and show them you can be trusted. You need to take the time to build relationships. If you don't do this, you're just another authority figure coming into people's lives and telling them what to do".

Time to build meaningful relationships is a luxury afforded to few social workers these days and Jonny understands that the constraints of modern ways of working often present a barrier to doing what is best by people. "It's like there's a choice between doing your paperwork or spending time with the people you came into this job to help" he lambasts. "If you decide to prioritise your paperwork, you marginalise the people you're writing about and do them a disservice. If you prioritise people, you have to accept that you'll get bollocked for not being up to date with recordings. Either way you're going to come out of it looking like a bad social worker, either in the eyes of your manager or the eyes of the people you're working for. It seems as if you either have to be in this job to write about people or be in this job to work with people. There's no way of doing both with the caseloads safeguarding social workers have. What a rubbish choice". It doesn't surprise me to see which choice Jonny made as he lets me know that "I'm notorious for my recordings being late and for never being in the office".

Having been involved in the care system for more than two thirds of his life, on both sides of the fence as man and boy, Jonny has seen a lot of changes in terms of the paperwork and procedures he fears restrict social workers from practising in a person-centred manner. "When computer systems came in we were promised that it would free social workers up to spend more time with people. We were told that everything would be quicker to do and information would be easier to access. Instead, we've seen social workers chained to our desks as the outcome of our work has become defined by what people can see on a computer screen instead of the real-life changes in those that we're supporting. There's this mantra that 'if it isn't recorded it didn't happen' so everyone's constantly trying to prove that they're efficient social workers who are making a difference. When social workers are spending most of the day at their desks and only a small part of it with people, you know something's fundamentally wrong with the system".

For as long as Jonny's been involved in the care system, he's seen an issue with social workers being prevented from spending time with people because of the need for ever-increasing accountability. Whenever a child's death has made national headlines because of perceived social work failings, the standard response from Labour and Conservative governments alike has been to implement reviews, regulations, legislation and new pieces of professional guidance. These political responses build up one at a time, layer after layer, in an effort to write away risk; civil servants and Members of Parliament believing that their efforts in Westminster can keep children safe in Carlisle, Dundee, Humberside. Such reactions to risk don't sit well with Jonny and he believes they belie a basic truth in social work that spending more time with people is key to keeping them safe. Looking back at his own time in the safeguarding system, it wasn't the social workers who were the most efficient or skilled in theoretical approaches that made the biggest difference to his life, it was the ones who had the time for him as a person and saw him more than just a case to get over the line for a tidy closure.

"I had no real lasting relationship with, or fond memories of, any social workers until the year 2000" Jonny tells me when exploring the importance of getting the time to build relationships. "Her name was Heidi and she had a massive impact on my life at a point where I was thinking about what to do after finishing my secondary education. She'd pick me up at the end of the school day and we'd do things together like go for a drive or get something to eat at a café. It never felt like she was working me as a case or trying to fix me. It just felt like she was a person who cared for me and could help me make the most of my life. She was the best social worker I'd ever had because she looked past the label of a 'looked after young person' and saw a young person just like everyone else instead". The irony of Jonny's adulation for Heidi is that, whilst she was the best social worker he'd worked with after seven years of being known to social services, she wasn't actually a social worker, at least not a qualified one who could legally use the protected title.

"The reason she had the time to get to know me and help me make the next steps in my life is that she was a student. Her low caseload meant she had the freedom to plan her work around what was best for young people like me, not try to fit us all in with everything else she was expected to do. When I think about that, how a student like Heidi was the best social worker I'd ever had at that point, it seems backwards. The same thing is still happening today where the people who are supposedly the least qualified are the ones spending the most time with people in need. It's got even worse since Heidi was a student and social workers are more like commissioners of care packages these days. It's the family support workers who do what I think social workers should be doing".

Those simple things that Heidi did for Jonny, like taking him to a McDonald's after school or coming to see him out of the blue just because she wanted to see how he was feeling, not because a statutory visit deadline was looming, saw him become more comfortable in opening up about his views, wishes and feelings. In turn, Heidi spending the time to gain Jonny's trust meant she could deliver better quality assessments that were more suited to his needs. Jonny believes that freeing social workers up to spend more time with people in this way is a win-win situation, with both the output of the professional's work and quality of service experienced by young people vastly improving as a result.

224

"Social workers want to be spending time with people, not sat at a desk trying to cover the backs of their managers in case something goes wrong. Our profession is full of some of the most wonderful and dedicated people you could ever meet. The problem is that the social workers who are best with people and care the most are often seen as poor because their reports and case note recordings are frequently late. I've seen the impact of this pressure to get everything on the system in social workers rushing through statutory visits in six minutes so they can head back to the office to get their recording done on time. This makes them look great on paper and shoots them to the top the performance indicator charts. Everyone seems to forget that those charts don't measure quality though, they only measure quantity".

As Jonny finished becoming 'looked after' and became a 'care leaver' instead, his personal advisor told him that the manager of the leaving care team, Howard, was looking to employ a care leaver within his team. Being in and out of the office on many occasions, Jonny had known Howard since he was sixteen years old and had seen the impact his vision for young people had on his workers like Heidi, as well as on young people in care such as himself. "Howard's focus was always on getting young people ready for life after care. He wanted us to be able to budget, to know how to cook healthy meals, to develop our social skills and to be prepared for the demands of independent living. With his focus on making sure people were ready for the rest of their lives, he thought it would be good to bring on-board a young person who'd been through his own team so they could provide a link between the service itself and the service users. My personal advisor encouraged me to apply for the job and I got it!"

"That time of my life was great. I had my first proper wage, got a place of my own and the job was brilliant. I was meeting councillors, helping to shape council policies and developing links with all the care leavers in the area to make sure their views were heard by the people paid to make decisions on their behalf. Howard was keen on progressing my career while I was in that role and saw the opportunity to give me skills that would see me through the rest of my life. He helped set me up with a qualification I could do alongside my work and pushed me to develop as a person. After eighteen months as a leaving care development worker, he wrote my reference for a family support worker's job in the same council who had looked after me since I was thirteen". Jonny got the job but he never forgot what Howard did for him. He's now the God-father to Jonny's oldest daughter and a lifelong mentor to Jonny himself.

A 21-year-old male who drove a 'boy racer' car and dressed in the same style of clothes as the young people he was working with, Jonny didn't fit the stereotypical family support worker mould. "It was a huge learning curve to step into that job" he reveals as he shares the leap up from a position that was created especially for someone like him, to a more formal job role that could be found in councils all over the country. "The good thing is that I was able to take my personality and experience into the job with me and learned I could use that to my advantage. Realising that I could be myself and draw on what I'd been through was a big turning point in my career. I learned that young people would respond to honesty more than me hiding behind a mask of professionalism".

The ability to be yourself and bring your own personality into work is something Jonny fears is being lost in contemporary social work, with practitioners scared of revealing anything about their personal lives for fear of compromising their professionality. "I used to try anything I could to make a breakthrough with people" he explains when laying out his more hands on and relationship-based approach to supporting families. "I'd have agreements in place such as taking young people out for a drive in my car if they went to school every day for a week. I'd share my own past stories to show young people that your background doesn't have to shape who you are. I'd go off plan and spend far more hours than I was supposed to doing direct work with parents to show them the impact that their drug use or domestic violence was having on their children".

On the subject of the plans that were in place for families he was supporting, Jonny admits that working alongside social workers could get frustrating. "It was sometimes hard to work other people's plans with families. I was the one spending more time with them than anybody else, yet I was working plans that were often five months old and made by people who might only see the children for half an hour once every fortnight. My focus was always on wanting to do more for families, but it was hard to do that when restrained by what was down as being needed as part of a child protection plan. That's when I started to learn that keeping children safe is about much more than what's written down on a piece of paper".

Despite those common frustrations about wishing he could do a little bit more for young people than he was allowed to, Jonny thrived in his family support role and ended up being managed by someone who used to be one of his social workers. "I was told right from the start that I'd come across confidential information about people that I'd grown up alongside in the care system" he explains. "It was never awkward though because I had good managers who set boundaries right from the start. Regardless of my own past, I was told 'we're all bound by the same rules' and given the same treatment as anyone else in the team". As well as succeeding in his work, Jonny's personal life was also blossoming. He fell in love with the woman he still adores to this day, they got a home together and he became a father. When talking about his daughter he looks back and laughs when he says "perhaps having a baby who never slept through the night wasn't the best time to start my social work career!"

The story that had taken him from a vulnerable boy picked up on his council's radar and taken into care because he was sleeping on the streets, through to a happy and successful family man who worked full-time for the same council, was to move onto its next chapter when Jonny was told about a secondment scheme that was offering Local Authority employees the chance to train as social workers. "If I hadn't been offered a secondment through the council there's no way I could have become a social worker" he explains to me when praising the opportunity he was given. "I had a house and a child, and we were reliant upon my wages. It would have been impossible to give up my job to study full-time. We couldn't have survived on student loans and bursaries alone". The secondment scheme that served him so well is something Jonny feels is a great loss to the system now that it has fallen out of fashion. "If you second people into social work they will end up staying in the council. They are people who live in the area, know the council and have years of practical experience about the reality of social work".

Jonny feels that many of the current issues that beset the national child protection workforce- a lack of experienced staff, high turnover, soaring sickness rates, increased reliance on agency workers- could be resolved by councils investing in their own workforce. Whether this is through bringing back the traditional secondment routes he went through, or introducing new apprenticeship schemes, he feels that councils growing their own workforces from within their local communities is sorely needed. Such moves are necessary if we are serious about resolving the national child protection recruitment crisis that sees many teams lacking experienced social workers. He also feels that these local schemes can open up the profession to people who were not encouraged by their parents to engage with education as children but will, if given the same chances he was, go on to shine as social workers later on in their lives.

"My secondment was like a golden ticket to me and it changed my whole life. I was in uni one day a week, had a day off to study and spent three days a week at work. All my tuition fees were paid, my books were bought for me and it gave me the financial freedom to support my family at the same time as training to be a social worker. Uni was amazing and I discovered that I loved studying so much. Funnily enough, the only things that I found a little bit hard going were the assignments on child protection because I knew about all of it already and was perhaps a little complacent at times".

The way Jonny talks about his time at university is a tonic to gee up even the most cynical and jaded critics of social work education. At the time I'm getting to know Jonny, over the spring months of 2017, there are great debates rumbling on about the future of social work training. Rumours abound that the social work bursary system is about to be scrapped in its entirety. The Scottish and Northern Irish social work regulators have announced that they will be preventing Frontline fast-track programme graduates from practising in adult services (McNicoll, 2017). Senior figures continue to argue the case for splitting the profession between specialisms at the point of entry to training, just as our multi-agency colleagues in health and education do with their degree-level programmes. Hearing Jonny's story about the joy at being given the opportunity to train as a social worker transcends these issues and shows the importance of making our profession accessible to all.

It's now some years on from Jonny's secondment and during the last of our four lengthy discussions he reveals that he got the manager's job he was thinking about applying for when I first sat down to listen to his story. He's looking forward to another step up within the same council who looked after him, trained him, employed him and helped make him the man he is today. "Over the years

I've seen for myself how essential strong leadership is for bringing about good outcomes in the lives of children" he tells me when recalling the life-changing impact that leaders like Paul and Howard have had during his time as a looked after child. "I think that's why there's such a difference between Local Authorities across the country. Even ones who shares the same boundaries and regional issues can be massively different in how well they care for the children that live within their borders. The ethics of senior managers and their interest in children as people, not just as cases or figures on a computer screen, is key to making a success of safeguarding. It's sad that austerity measures and budget cuts have meant leaders have a harder time in balancing the books, but they still have choices to make about how they spend the money that's left over and how they use it to shape their services. I'm lucky because North Yorkshire have done it right".

I ask Jonny to explain how he feels the Local Authority that raised him as man and boy has 'done it right' and he goes on to set out the forward-thinking approach that means he would never dream about working anywhere else. "When the budget cuts came in, our Director and Assistant Director made keeping social work teams together a priority. Our council took pride in the fact that all our teams were made up of permanent workers and there was very little turnover in the workforce".

"They wanted to try and keep things this way because they saw how important it was for children to have the same social workers and not go through lots of changes. Listening to social workers, they found out that one of the biggest problems in our work was the old-fashioned computer system that was slowing down everything we were trying to achieve. They wanted to listen to social workers and free us up from dated computer systems but were told it was going to cost millions to do so. It was a difficult case to make for investing in your workforce when your budget is being cut in half. But they went away and worked out that poor IT systems were

230

costing the council far more than it would cost to replace them. The wasted time of inefficient working was leading to thousands of hours being lost every week. It wasn't a productive way of working at all. So, they invested in a new recording system, gave us all smart phones and provided everyone with touch-screen tablet computers that mean we can work from anywhere we need to".

Jonny describes a typical day at work to show me the impact that forward-thinking leaders implementing modern technology has had on social workers in his area. "You'll get a referral in and can access all of the past details of the family on your tablet, wherever you are. You can then visit the family and when you need to get signed consent for information sharing, you can pull up the forms on your tablet and use the stylus for parents to sign it there and then. You can then file that completed form straight away. When you do direct work obtaining children's views you can pull up a three houses template on the screen and ask them to fill in their hopes, worries and dreams by using your 'magic pen' stylus. Again, you can file it and save it to their records straight away. If you've got a meeting later in the day you can type up the minutes as you go along, ask if you can stay back in the room for ten minutes, get them completed and file them straight away. There's not the rush to get back to the office and get your work on the system. Having a tablet pc connected straight to your network through a smart phone means you save so much time".

As I look at my own work phone, a Nokia 'brick' that isn't too far removed from the first mobile phone I ever owned in 1999, and think about all the slow and ageing computers I've been forced to endure in the workplace, I can't help but feel a little bit jealous about the efficient way of working Jonny describes. He thinks we can go much further in utilising technology in social work though. "How much easier would it be if we were allowed to do things like take pictures, videos and voice recordings in our work? What better way would there be to capture a child's journey than by recording and sharing the views of the children we're trying to protect? It would be incredible to be able to show a judge, during care proceedings, a picture of home conditions rather than a written description which might miss out the sheer magnitude of the situation at the time. It would save a lot of time in proceedings and cut out the idea that social workers lie or put words into children's mouths".

Jonny's come a long way in his life and his circumstances are far removed from what he shares with me about his early years. For all those changes, I get a sense that he still retains the same desire to challenge injustice that saw him fight to get his sibling living with him when he first went into care twenty years ago. These days he's no longer having to fight for his sibling, who's big enough and old enough to look after themself now, but he devotes his life to fighting on behalf of other young people instead. On a local level as a soon-to-be manager in the leaving care service, to a national level as a trustee for a National Voice, he's doing whatever he can to make the changes that care experienced young people so desperately need. "Not righting my own wrongs through them" he reminds me, "but making changes for them".

Chapter Eighteen: How was your day at work?

How was your day at work?

For everyone that has a parent, spouse, significant other, child or someone that cares about them, I'm sure you've been asked this question many times in your life.

I ask my three-year-old son how his day was, every day, and typically it's full of things like playing outside, taking a nap, new toys and adventures at preschool. My spouse will talk about difficulties with a co-worker, being tired due to working hard, and his boss being tough on him. We typically talk about frustrations because that's the way it is for most of us, we focus on the negatives first. It's not always bad news though, and other times when we've had happier days we'll find the time to talk about our successes or exciting things that have happened during our ten hours apart.

When the question is put to me, my answer is usually either "it was a good day today" or "today wasn't good". That's about all I can say on the matter. My occupation as a child welfare worker makes it hard to discuss my day for many reasons. Confidentiality being number one, but mostly because people that don't experience the same things I do may find it hard to listen to what I have to put up with, or give me the "I don't know how you do what you do, I could never do that" speech that, for all their well-meaning intentions, can feel a little patronising.

Today I've decided to touch on why I do what I do.

Over the past eight years that I've done this job, the experiences I've had have been everything from utterly amazing to downright terrifying. Things are often good, but often really bad too.

I've been exposed to methamphetamine fumes. I've seen meth labs dismantled in front of me from a few feet away. It makes me physically ill. I've had headaches and nausea from exposure to the noxious meth fumes, often to the point where it's hard to carry on throughout my day. Please don't feel sorry for me though. My exposure means that I'm able to move children who live in that environment out of that environment; helping them breathe fresh air and stop being sick. It's not a terrible thing that I was exposed, it's a good thing the children are no longer exposed.

I have taken children from their moms and dads; screaming, crying, not understanding why. Other times they go with me without any resistance at all, because they're willing to trust that a stranger might keep them safer than their parents ever could. I buy them McDonald's because they haven't eaten. I drive to Walmart and buy formula, diapers and bottles. I feed the babies in my office, change full diapers, get peed on, and scavenge for clean clothes to put them in. Children come in with lice. I treat them by putting on gloves, picking through their hair, and spraying treatment on their heads. Don't feel sorry for me. It was all worth it because they're fed, clothed, treated and sent to a safe home.

I've sat on couches that have had cockroaches crawling next to me. I've been bitten by fleas. Don't feel bad for me. Because of those bites I've been able to get someone into the house to treat those bugs and the kids now sleep soundly at night. I've been in homes that gag me with their smell and others I cannot walk through because of clutter. I've been in homes that are freezing because of no heat, and homes that have no utilities at all. I help families remedy this. Their kids are now warm, clean and have their needs met because I'm willing to walk in there on my own.

I've sat at the hospital for hours on end with children who've been hurt by their own parents. I've rocked and fed babies that were born addicted to drugs, who are attached to so many cords that you're afraid to move too much in case one falls out. I've ventured into dirty bedrooms to find kids whose parents have abandoned them, so I've picked them up in a small carrier and drove them hours away to a safe home where they can be cared for. I fall in love with each and every one of these children I come across. I leave them behind with a little tear knowing that the new family caring for them will make sure they don't hurt anymore. That they're no longer pumped full of drugs, assaulted or left to fend for themselves.

I act as a mom, a friend, a counsellor, a bad guy, a good guy, a helper. Kids tell me things and wait for my face to react. When it doesn't, they tell me more. Often times a four-year-old will tell me things that most fifteen-year olds don't know and don't see. They watch my face for a reaction because they're used to that. When I don't react, they trust. They tell me more. It breaks my heart. It scares me for my own son. But I don't react. And they tell me more. Teenagers call me and talk to me as if I was their parent. And in some situations, I'm the closest thing they have to one. In reality I'm a complete stranger who's only there because of my job. But I listen. I listen and I care. I listen, care and make changes for them.

I've had nights where I've cried myself to sleep, wondering if I did the right thing or if I could have done more. I've had nights where I've celebrated because a child found a permanent safe forever home. I've had nights where I wished I could shout to the world that I got through to a family and they changed, and the kids are safe and happy because of it.

These tales of mine are nothing special in this job. My co-workers all have very similar stories. We share them during the day. We laugh, we cry, we yell, we scream and we bond over what we've been through. Child welfare workers all over America do the same things that I do and some have seen far worse than I ever will. In the office we often say "we should write a book, but no one would believe it". Well, here is just a glimpse into many of my days and I hope you do believe it because every word of it is true. While it's not in detail, it's enough to explain why I do what I do.

Social work is hard. I don't know if I can, or will, do it forever. But, for now, I do it with everything that I have in me. It drains me and fills me up at the same time. Someone has to do this job and keep these kids safe and, today, I'm glad I do.

Chapter Nineteen: Natasha's story

"One day there was a knock on the door"

Those nine words that Natasha starts her story with will be all too familiar to the millions of parents out there who have, at one time or another, had to face up to the dread of a stranger calling at their home and asking to speak to them about their children. As a social worker myself, I've often been on the other side of that door. I am the one who knocks. But in my time with Natasha we speak not as professionals and service users, but as two human beings.

"There was a lady standing there who said she was from social services and wanted to talk to me about something. She didn't tell me anything more than that on the doorstep. When she came in and sat down she told me a little bit more, that they'd had a report from the police about domestic abuse and were concerned about my children. I didn't expect it at all. I didn't even know how they'd found out about what was going on. I'd called the police but I'd never called the social".

In the years since that first fateful knock on her door, Natasha has become an expert by experience of child protection procedures. Seeing things from the 'other side' to a social worker like me, she's got insight and knowledge that I'll never have. Even the most empathetic and caring of professionals will never truly know what it must really feel like to have that knock on the door and know that your parenting ability is under the spotlight. For all the experience that she has now though, Natasha admits to feeling "woefully naïve" when she first realised she had become "known to social services".

"If I'm being honest, that first visit didn't really make any difference at all" Natasha recalls as her mind wanders back to a moment in time that would go on to change her entire life. "I was nineteen, I had no one there to support me and the social worker didn't explain things in a way that I could understand. The importance of what that visit meant and the concerns the social worker had about my children were totally lost on me. All I'd ever known was the life I was leading and the formal world of social work was like nothing I'd ever come across before. Looking back, I didn't stand a chance of navigating that system by myself as a young mum with two kids to look after and an abusive partner to keep at bay".

"He started to hurt me when I became pregnant with our first child together" Natasha tells me, her voice quaking as she recalls what she was subjected to during a period of her life when most young couples' days would have been filled with excitement about the new little person they were bringing into the world. "My dad abused my mum, so what he was doing seemed normal to me. Some of my very first memories were of witnessing domestic violence, so the fact it was happening to me came as no real surprise. I'd grown up to learn that men hit women and you had to tolerate it".

"When it first started happening, him hurting me like he did, I told my mum about what was happening in the hope that she'd give me the confidence to leave or some scraps of advice that might help calm him down when he set at me. Instead of offering me any comfort or compassion, she said it was my fault. Her exact words were 'well, you do wind him up'. Getting nowhere with my mum, I went back to submitting to his abuse until I built up the courage to speak out about it again. This time I went to one of my closest friends and told her about everything- the physical assaults, the psychological abuse, the domination- all of it. Her response was to tell me 'everyone goes through that' and she brushed it off as if nothing had been said at all. I was left feeling that if my mum blamed me and my friend thought it was normal, then what he was doing couldn't be that bad. It went on and on and on".

"The PTSD that I live with makes some of my memories from back then a little bit hazy, which means it's hard to remember just how many times he hurt me. But when it got really bad, when I was seriously scared for myself and the babies, I'd call the police". The babies Natasha speaks of were a little girl who was a toddler at the time when the vicious cycle of abuse and subsequent police call outs began in earnest, who had a different father, and an infant daughter who had begun to suffer exposure to her father's abusive ways many months before she had even left the sanctuary of her mother's womb.

Natasha describes a played-out scene where violence would flare and she'd take preventative action to protect herself and her two children. "I'd call the police, they'd arrest him, then lead him away in handcuffs down to the station. The next morning, after he'd spent a night cooling off in the cells, I'd get a phone call from an officer saying he had nowhere else to go and asking me if he could come back home. Every single time I said yes". That lack of further action from the police, compounded by her childhood experiences and lack of support from family and friends, further entrenched Natasha's belief that what she was going through was the norm. Sadly, statistics showing the common prevalence of domestic abuse throughout the land demonstrate that Natasha was far from alone in accepting that a violent relationship was to be endured. In England and Wales alone, two women a week are murdered by their partners; one in four of all women will experience some form of domestic abuse in their lifetimes (Women's Aid, 2017).

Natasha is the human story behind one of those statistics. Her children are the human story behind care applications going before the courts at an ever-increasing rate. Her abusive partner is the human story behind figures that show domestic violence is the least likely crime to be reported to the police and therefore the most likely crime for perpetrators to get away with (Office for National Statistics, 2016).

"I didn't realise that every time the police attended and saw there were children present, they passed on information to social services" Natasha tells me when thinking back to the days before social workers became part and parcel of her daily life. "If I'm being honest, part of me is glad that I didn't know because I think the fear of losing the kids might have stopped me from calling the police as often as I did. I guess that's why the police don't make it clear that they share information with social workers. It would scare some people off from ever ringing 999".

"After that first visit from a social worker, nothing really changed at all. The system wasn't explained, none of the words she was using made any sense and I was left without a clue as to what she expected of me. Even when the meetings began and reports started coming through, the severity of what was happening was never properly explained. It was like they expected me to know what the technical terms they were using meant or to have the capacity, as an abused nineteen-year-old mother of two young kids, to suddenly turn my life around with no practical help at all. There were a lot of meetings and plenty of reports about me, but there was very little in the way of real world help to turn things around back then. Maybe they were expecting my family to help, but didn't realise that mum was condoning what he was doing to me. Maybe they were relying on me to do it on my own, but didn't realise the total and utter control this man had over every inch of me".

"Even after months and months of meetings, with a few different

240

social workers coming and going over that time, the fact that my children were at stake never really dawned on me. I was still in a relationship with Gary, the abuse went on as if nothing had ever changed and fortnightly visits from a social worker were offering a single hour of respite in the eye of a storm of abuse that continued to rage on and on. It was just paperwork and people talking at meetings. That's all social services intervention was to me".

"About eight months after that first knock at the door, a child protection conference took place and, as usual, everyone had their say about my life and what I should be doing to keep my daughters safe. The social worker at the time asked me to stay back at the end of the meeting because her manager wanted to come in and have a word with me. That's when I was read the riot act. The manager told me there and then that 'if you don't leave Gary, the only option we'll have left is to take the children out of your care'. I know she was doing that for the right reason, to keep my babies safe, but it felt badly handled. I was put under pressure to kick him out of my house that same day or face the threat of losing my children if I didn't".

"I went home, all by myself and without anybody to support me if he kicked off, and asked Gary to leave there and then. I now realise just how much risk I was at by doing that alone. Many women just like me are killed at the point where they show the confidence to end a relationship. I could have been one of them. But when I told him to go, he did. The only thing he asked was for the time to pack his bags and leave me a letter explaining how he felt. After he left, I sat and read the letter. It told me all about how sorry he was for what he'd put me through and how he promised he was going to change. There wasn't anything about the kids in there, it was all about him".

"He came back six hours later and started banging on the door in the middle of the night. The kids shared a bedroom on the ground floor, next to the front door, and his hammering was causing them to stir. Faced with a choice between letting him wake the children up or letting him in, I felt letting him in was the only sensible option. If I called the police it might look like I hadn't carried through on my promise to the social worker's manager and I'd lose the kids either way. Instead I reasoned that I could let him in, hear him out, and calm him down before sending him on his way again in the morning. I opened the door".

When people who've never suffered at the hands of a perpetrator imagine abusive men, I've found that they tend to picture burly types with tattoos and scars. They conjure up images of thuggish oafs with dangerous dogs who drink heavily and live criminal lifestyles. What they don't do is realise that people from all walks of life are capable of committing the most heinous acts of violence and abuse against the people that they should care about the most. They don't picture men like me, ordinary run of the mill guys, being capable of murdering their partners and children. Perhaps that's a good thing, that we haven't lost all our innocence to the point where we suspect that everyone we know and love is capable of monstrous deeds. However, people like Natasha know all too well that the old caricature images of outwardly thuggish men being abusive partners is far from the truth.

"He wasn't your typical bad boy thug. He was very clever. He was very articulate" she tells me when turning her mind back to the days when Gary had total dominion over every single aspect of her being. "He told me how he knew he could beat the system that social workers were part of. He managed to convince me that there was a police state conspiracy for social services to control the lives of people like me and him. He used to talk about 'state involvement in our lives' and would blame the fact social workers were assessing us for his violent tempers. The blame for what he was doing and how he was acting was pushed towards social workers and it was apparently their fault that he would 'lose it' with me. I believed him".

"The same day they found out he was back in the home was the same day they told me that they were applying to court to have the children taken from our care. We had a few days' notice to prepare for the hearing. I didn't tell anyone at all what was happening. Part of me was embarrassed to reveal the truth, but a bigger part of me still believed that Gary could beat the system that was putting so much pressure on him. On the day of the hearing he went to court by himself and I stayed at home to look after the kids. I kept myself busy, I tried to keep my mind occupied with other things, but I still wasn't as worried as I should have been. I still believed that Gary could beat the system. That was how much control he had over my mind".

"When he rang me, all that he said was 'they are coming to take them away at half past four'".

"As soon as he hung up, I calmly started packing my daughters' clothes and belongings into little bags so they would be ready to go when the social worker came to take them away from me. There weren't any tears or tantrums. I didn't break down. I simply started doing the practical things I needed to make sure the kids were ready to leave when that knock on the door came in less than an hour's time. You see, the abuse from Gary had been getting worse and worse in the run up to court. He'd get mad at 'the system', then take out his rage on me. He'd get frustrated at not being able to control social workers with his threats, then punish me as a result. Then after the beatings, he'd say sorry and push the blame back onto social services for making him so angry again".

"The reason why I was calm when the news came through was because, as hard as this is to admit now, I was actually glad the children were being taken away from me. I had prepared for it happening and, deep down in my heart, I knew it was what was best for them at that time. His abuse had been getting worse for months and I hoped that the children being taken away would stop some of it, that It would give me a break from being a mum for a little while. He had ground me down so much that I ended up blaming being a parent for everything that was happening. I reasoned that, if the kids weren't there, he wouldn't have a reason to be angry with me and the cycle of abuse might finally come to an end. I felt that I didn't need a break from him at that point, that I just needed a break from being a mum. The children being taken away would give me that chance".

"My two girls were all dressed up and waiting with their little bags of toys and clothes when a pair of social workers turned up in tandem with the police. I know they were 'just doing their jobs' but I wished they'd have given me the one and only thing I asked for when they came to take my girls away from me, a single minute alone with my babies. I only wanted to say goodbye. I just wanted to have a moment to say that I loved them and would miss them. Instead I was told that this couldn't happen and met with stony faces at a time when a tiny shred of human kindness would have meant everything to me".

"And then I was left all alone".

As Natasha takes a break in her story, it's clear that we're both fighting back the tears. For Natasha, it's because she's pulling out old memories that have lain dormant for years and is being reminded of the worst time in her life. For me, it's because I've been the social worker in situations like that before, and the memories of being the one who knocks come flooding back to me.

I've taken new born babies from their parents and handed them over to strangers in hospital waiting rooms. I've stood on opposing sides of courtrooms, across from mothers who have dragged themselves out of hospital beds to fight for the right to take their day-old children back home with them; stitched up and leaking breastmilk whilst trying to get their head around the legal complexities they are being faced with. I've had to try and search for the words that might bring a single crumb of comfort to children who are being taken out of the only homes they have ever known and ferried away to live with strangers.

These things have brought me no joy, even though they were all necessary to keep children safe. Every single time I took a child into care was followed by a sleepless night where I lay awake thinking how the children were settling down in their new beds and how the parents were coping with their empty nests. I might have been on opposite sides from parents in the courtroom, and we may have disagreed on what was in their children's best interests, but we were all human at the end of the day. If my life had taken a different path then it might have been me fighting for the right to take my baby back home from hospital with me. If I'm beset by issues in future, I could end up begging a social worker to take a chance on me showing that I'm capable of making the changes they're asking for.

For all the labels of 'service user' and 'professional' that the nature of our job dictates we must apply, at the end of the day we are all just people trying to get by in this world. Everybody is the hero in their own story. Everybody believes that they are doing the right thing. The social workers coming to take Natasha's daughters into care believed they were doing the right thing because she had clearly failed to protect them from the significant emotional harm of being repeatedly exposed to domestic abuse. The severity of harm and evidence base was there to put this before a judge and get a decision. That fact doesn't make it any less hard on Natasha or any easier for social workers trying to cope with the trauma of removal. Her recollection brings back memories of all the times I've had to hide my own emotions behind a façade of coolness whilst carrying out the duties placed upon me as an agent of the state.

Catching her breath and managing to hold back the tears, Natasha continues by telling me how "shortly after Gary came back from court, the police turned up and arrested him for assaulting me the week before, knowing he would be in the house after the hearing earlier in the day. As much as he deserved that, it left me totally isolated and all alone. Without even the kids there for company, I realised that night how he was the only person I could turn to. He was the only person in my life. He must have realised that he had totally broken my spirit and that I was now wholly dependent upon him because, after the girls left, the physical abuse got worse than it had ever been before".

"They were taken away on the 28th of July and I tried my best to keep going. I fought to keep myself alive. I managed to hold on until the 11th of December".

"I don't remember what started him off that night. It's hard to pick out one thing when it was happening so often. I just remember that it ended with him holding me down on the floor with both hands gripped around my neck, getting tighter and tighter. I felt the world slipping away from me. I felt myself fading out. Just as I was losing my hold on life he let go, calmly stood up and told me that he would go and wait outside until the police turned up. He did exactly as he'd promised and once again they came and took him away for the night. Once again, I was left alone. That was the first time I took an overdose to try and end my own life".

"In the four and a half months whilst my girls were gone, he'd made me believe that I was to blame for everything that had happened, his anger turning from me and his lost battle with the state, to me alone. In the aftermath of that night's attack, the worst one yet, I started to believe that if I was gone then maybe he could take care of the girls himself. It was me that he was violent with, me who the kids witnessed getting hurt, me to blame for everything. I counted out twenty paracetamol tablets by the time I lost track of how many I was putting into my mouth and swallowing down".

Natasha was well known to her local police force, with callouts to her home a regular occurrence and Gary a frequent occupant of their cells. Following a pattern that had been long established, they called Natasha to give an update on their handling of Gary's arrest and to keep her in the loop about the next steps they would be taking. Every other time this would happen, Gary would tell the police he had nowhere else to go and Natasha would feel under pressure to take him back. Once again, his excuses, apologies and false promises of wanting to be a better man would come pouring out in a successful effort to break her will one more time.

"This time when they called, I didn't answer" Natasha explains to me. "This time I was passed out and dying. When they called to give an update and there was no answer, they knew something was up. I'd answered every other time they'd called and would always speak to them about what was happening with Gary. They knew something was wrong when I didn't pick up the phone that night. Thankfully they decided to act on their suspicion and take the time to come and check on me".

The first paramedic on the scene told the attending officers that Natasha's condition was so severe that she was going to die. This resulted in the police setting up a cordon around the property

247

and stationing officers outside the front entrance to preserve the scene. Their expectation was that a forensics team would be arriving once the confirmation came through from hospital that Natasha had passed away.

"Before then, I'd always been seen as a risk because of what I was allowing my children to see and for letting myself be the victim of domestic abuse" Natasha shares as she explains the aftermath of her first suicide attempt. "The risk came from what was being done to me, not really what I was doing myself. But coming so close to killing myself and those terminal thoughts turning into actions meant that the social worker started seeing me as more of a risk. Words like 'unstable' and 'suicidal ideation' started to appear in reports as my reaction to everything I was going through was assessed as being irrational. Instead of giving up, it was made clear that I should have been doing more to fight for my children and be the mum they deserved. That just made me feel like even more of a failure".

"After I was discharged from hospital I told Gary that was the end of us, and this time he gave up without a fight. Maybe it was because he realised how close he'd come to killing me. Maybe it was because he knew how close I'd come to killing myself. Either way he listened to me and stayed away. I'm glad he made that decision because I'm not sure if, even after coming so close to dying, I'd have had the courage to end it for good back then. Shortly after he moved out I realised I needed a fresh start and I had to get away from the town where all these terrible things had happened to me. I moved to a different county to start all over again. It meant going from seeing my girls three times a week to once every month, but I had to do it otherwise they wouldn't have had a mum to see at all".

As Natasha recounts her story to me, an experienced child protection social worker who has sadly seen situations like hers far too often, I find myself getting increasingly frustrated about how little she seems to remember in relation to the processes and procedures underpinning everything she is telling me. At first, I put her lack of clarity down to the PTSD she reveals can make memories of the past difficult to pin down. But as we speak more often and become closer, it begins to dawn on me that Natasha simply wasn't informed of the magnitude of what she was going through. My knowledge helps fill in the gaps and identify that the vague 'meetings' she describes will be core groups, child protection conferences, public law outline meetings, looked after care teams and the like. My experience teaches me that the blanket 'paperwork' she remembers will have been initial assessments, core group minutes, child protection plans, core assessments, looked after plans, parenting assessments and all the other assorted *accoutrements* that accompany the safeguarding processes that shape modern day social work.

But to Natasha they are simply meetings and paperwork.

In social work, we can often become numbed to the power of what we do. We enter the profession with years of training telling us all about empowerment, anti-oppressive practice, legal frameworks and our role as agents of the state. Over time, these essential aspects of the role that once seemed so mystical soon become the humdrum reality of our daily lives. The jobs that we were once so worried about ever getting in the first place become ones that we take for granted and dream of leaving when the going gets tough. The small pieces of observed practice that we nervously performed for our supervisors on placement- homes visits, chairing meetings and undertaking direct work with service users- become part and parcel of our daily lives. We soon settle into routines and normality sets in where we once found nervous excitement.

Natasha's account is a reminder to all of us that we must never take what we do for granted. Even if this is our thousandth 'meeting' or the hundredth time we have picked up a 'case' where domestic violence is putting children at risk of emotional abuse, we should be mindful that the people we are serving do not know the system like we do. We should never let the individuals we support believe that our assessments and reviews are nothing but 'reports' and 'meetings'. It is vital that people know the importance of what is happening, the processes that social workers follow, the laws that shape our practice and, most importantly, how we can all work together within these guidelines to help bring about improvements.

The move away from the area that had brought her so much pain was good for Natasha and, for the first few months at least, she found the space needed to start pulling her life back together again. "Although I wasn't seeing the girls as much, it was working out okay for me" Natasha explains as she recalls how it felt to move away for a fresh start. "Gary would sometimes contact me, but it wasn't about us getting back together or anything, just about seeing our daughter and asking how she was doing. Then one day he rang about seeing her and casually mentioned that he knew where the foster carer lived. I tried to move the conversation on but he wouldn't let his point go and started talking about a plan to snatch the girls back. I was in a panic and didn't know what else to do, so I said I'd find the money for him to come up and see me. The idea was to try and talk him out of this plan he was hatching to take the girls away from their foster carers and go on the run".

"I paid for his travel to come see me and, even though some time had passed from the phone call about him knowing where the girls were living, he was still set on this idea of us all going on the run. The feeling that the state was against all of us was still on his mind and he continued to believe that he could outsmart them. I didn't want anything to do with it and tried to tell him so, but he wouldn't listen and started getting more and more angry at my efforts to talk him out of his plan. In the end, I went back to something that I'd had to do many times in the past to stop him working himself up to the point where he'd hurt me. I did what I promised I'd never do again and I slept with him".

"Two months later I found out that I was pregnant. I cried and cried and cried. I cried my eyes out. I'm so ashamed of what I had to do and the power he still had over me, despite everything he'd done to me and all that I'd lost because of him. My son must never find out how he was conceived".

"The pregnancy went well but, falling between the care of two different councils- the one where I was living and the one where my children were in care- meant that there wasn't really any support for me during the pregnancy. I was left in the dark about what was going to happen until two weeks before my due date when I was told that I'd be moving into a mother and baby placement with my son when he arrived. I supposed that was better than the alternative of him being taken away from me as soon as he was born".

"The birth itself was fine and, with having had two before, the midwives would have let me go the next day. That wasn't the case this time because there was no placement ready for me to be discharged on time. I instead had to sit and watch all the other parents happily take their little bundles of joy home with them while I lay in bed waiting for a place to be found for us. It ended up taking four days. When a placement was found for me, what should have been a chance for me to prove myself as a mother turned into a nightmare".

"In my past involvement with social services, when plans had been set out to me they tended to be a bit unclear in terms of what they were asking. This time it was very different and I was set a clear list of what I had to achieve to show that I had changed as a mum. I had to complete a domestic violence awareness course, go through therapy, take part in parenting programmes and show everyone that I could always keep my son safe from harm. They weren't giving me any leeway and it felt like I was only ever one slip away from losing him".

"It felt like I was being set up to fail. I had all these things I had to do for the sake of my son, but nobody to look after him so I could focus on what was being asked of me. I'd moved away from all my friends and family, had no money for childcare and the foster carer wouldn't look after him by herself. To make matters worse, my new GP decided to take me off my antipsychotic medication which meant that I was having to cope without them propping me up any more. Life in my placement was getting more and more difficult too as I had no privacy or space to myself. I wasn't even allowed to have my bedroom door closed. That led to many moments when the foster carer would walk in as I as getting dressed. It was degrading".

"One morning I told the foster carer that I was going out for a walk with my son and instead I ended up taking him to see my mum. I asked if she could have him for a little while as there was something important that I had to do. She was happy to spend some time alone with her grandson, so I left him there as I went to find the nearest supermarket to stock up on nappies and formula milk. I wanted to make sure he had the things that he needed when I was dead".

"That last attempt at suicide might not have killed me, but it did take me to rock bottom. I'd had three children and now none of them were in my care. The only thing that gave me a bit of hope when I woke up in hospital was the news that my son was going to live with my parents".

"When you've got a child in your care, you get help thrown at you left, right and centre. Even though you might not always want what's being offered or agree with the views people have of you, there is support out there. That all changes when you're no longer seen as capable of looking after your own kids. Instead of going into a nice family home or being helped with finding a place of my own, I was discharged from hospital as homeless and ended up in a hostel".

"For all my worry about what that hostel would be like and the people I'd be living with, the staff there gave me the security and support to start learning how to live all over again. I got a part-time job delivering takeaways and registered with my old GP who put me back on the medication that had helped me in the past. Being back where I knew people and having my own space, even if it was in a hostel, was such a help in finding myself again. Having a job was a real bonus too. It brought order to my life, settled me in a routine and gave me a reason to get out of bed and get dressed".

"Just as things were settling down for me and I was starting to feel a little bit like myself again, the legal process for my son began. I knew the way things worked by now and how the system needed to find a permanent solution for him, just as they had by sorting out my eldest daughter living with her dad and my other daughter being with my parents. I knew this was something we had to go through. I was prepared for it and felt I was in a better place to face the stresses and strains that come with being put before a judge and argued about by solicitors. Don't get me wrong, it still scared me a bit, but not half as much as knowing that I'd have to face Gary did".

I've been a social worker long enough to know that you can't take anything for granted. From unforeseen disasters when you think everything is going well, to people who make unbelievably positive changes when everyone else but you has written them off, you can never really predict what is going to happen in the lives of those you're working with. That's not just the case for social work though, we human beings are unpredictable in our nature and the thing that makes our time on earth so special is that you never quite know what's going to happen tomorrow. This is one of the reasons why practitioners who are more person-centred tend to find such frustration in many modern systems that reduce the lives of human beings to ticking boxes on a computer screen. Sometimes humans do things that no amount of evidence-based practice can predict. Sometimes life throws up miracles that not even the most rigid of risk assessments can anticipate.

Many people who haven't been social workers would have written Natasha off at this point in her life. Hell, many people who have been social workers will have probably done the same but would have used a term like 'lacks capacity to change' instead of 'written off'. Then something happened next that nobody could have predicted. No social worker had planned this intervention, no professional had prescribed this treatment and not even Natasha herself had envisaged this outcome.

She fell in love.

"Having to face Gary in court and argue about our children was getting on top of me. One day it came to a head and I broke down in tears during the middle of a hearing. I got upset and ran out of the courtroom and into the arms of a security guard. He didn't tell me to go back into the courtroom or ignore me in case he got into trouble at work. Instead he let keep clinging onto him and took me to a quiet room where I could try and pull myself together. He didn't say anything or even ask me any questions. He just lis-

254

tened. I'd gotten so used to people asking me personal questions or telling me what I had to do, that I'd forgotten how good it could feel to have somebody just let you open up to them".

"We didn't have a lot of time together, because I had to go back into court and finish off, but I couldn't stop thinking about that man. I don't think there are many people who've been through what I have who want to go to court for fun, but the next day I went back to see if I could thank that stranger who'd given me something nobody else had for years, the time to be myself".

"I found him and gave him my phone number. We've been together even since".

"Things were settled in court, with my son staying with my parents. Knowing that my kids were happy and settled with family was a big relief and it felt like I could focus on repairing all the damage that Gary had done to me. He no longer held any power over me and this time I really could move on. This time I wasn't having to do it alone. For all the help social workers tried to give me, they had lots of other children to think about and had their own lives they went back to. When Steve finished work, he came home to me. Steve was everything that Gary wasn't. He was everything that any woman could have wanted".

I never meet Steve myself, but the way Natasha gushes about him leaves me feeling a little weak at the knees and I must admit to developing a bit of a man crush on this guy. He sounds like a hero and, to Natasha at least, he was a knight in shining armour who came to her in her hour of need.

"Contact was going really well with my kids when I found out I was pregnant, but there was still a social worker looking over things to see if it would work out okay in the end" Natasha recalls as she builds up to the point where her youngest child Freya was born. "This time I wanted to do things on my terms and not have to wait until I was due to give birth before finding out what was happening with my baby, so I paid for an early scan to confirm the pregnancy a few weeks after the positive test. When I saw the images on the scan and was told everything was looking fine, I took the pictures along to the next contact and asked for a quiet word with the social worker at the end. Wanting to do things my way, and not have things done to me, I showed her the scan picture and asked her to self-refer me".

"They waited a little while and, not long after my second proper scan at the hospital, a social worker came out to do an assessment on me and Steve. Things felt different this time round. Instead of hearing about what I'd done wrong and what needed to be changed, I was hearing about what I was doing well and how I could be supported in maintaining those positive changes. Instead of feeling like I was being told off for my failures, I was getting praised for the work I'd put in to make things better. It was the first time I'd ever felt hopeful about a meeting with a social worker. The assessment she wrote backed up what she'd said in person and me and Steve felt that the baby was going to be coming home from hospital with us. Having something in writing that said I could be a good mum was such an important thing".

"That social worker was the first one who ever took the time to explain things to me. I learned that what she'd done was called a core assessment and that she'd be passing on my work to another team who would be helping us with a child in need plan until the baby was born. The next social worker was called Rachel and she was brilliant. Open, lovely, honest. A really lovely person who wanted to make sure me and Steve had all the help we needed to look after the baby".

"Freya was born in February and in May they wanted to close the case. Everyone thought that I'd be over the moon at that news, but I wasn't. Rachel had done so much for me that I didn't want her to go. I begged them to keep the case open for a few more months, just until Freya was a little bit older and I knew me and Steve could manage. Rachel's manager said yes and she stayed on a little bit longer until I was ready to say bye on my own terms, when I knew I was ready".

By the time I get to know Natasha, Freya's case has been closed and it's the first time in four years that she hasn't been 'known to social services'. Contact with her older children is happening more frequently than ever and the next step is to look at moving it to unsupervised. Freya is coming on beautifully and looks like the happiest little girl you could ever hope to meet. Her and Steve's relationship is as loving as ever. She has what she jokingly refers to as her first "proper job". She is the happiest she has ever been.

Natasha has come a long way from that tragic night when a para-medic told a police officer to prepare her home as a scene for a forensic investigation because she was likely going to die. As much as a little part of me hopes that some credit for the positive changes she's made will be given to social workers, I know what she's going to tell me when I ask her what she thinks gave her the power to finally make the changes she needed to safely care for her children. "If it wasn't for Steve, I wouldn't be here today" she tells me. "He's been so stable and supportive. He doesn't have a bad bone in his body. In a year, I went from being homeless to having a proper job and a roof over my head. The most impor-tant thing for people with mental health problems is stability. Steve gave me that".

Steve's love gave Natasha the power to feel like she wasn't alone and afforded her the security of knowing that she no longer had to do it all by herself. So much of what we deal with in social work comes down to the lack of love or the misplaced and damaging feelings that such a powerful emotion can evoke. From domestic violence caused by fits of jealous rage driven by unrequited love and children being sexually abused by adults they've been groomed to believe they are in love with, through to maternal and paternal love triumphing through even the most difficult of times, so much of what we face in social work is tinged with the emotion of love. We can't create it as an intervention or set it as a target to be achieved as part of a plan, but it's something so powerful that we need to be aware of it in this line of work.

As I say my final goodbyes to Natasha, acutely aware that she doesn't need another social worker hanging around for too much longer, I'm reminded of a quote from Orson Welles that I read many years before I even thought about entering this profession:

"We're born alone, we live alone, we die alone. Only through love and friendship can we create the illusion for the moment that we're not alone".

I leave Natasha safe in the knowledge that she's no longer fighting her battles alone.

Chapter Twenty: A new hope

As I sit here and try to bring this book to a close in September 2017, it feels like social work is going through a tough time. In the United Kingdom, where I live and work, there are clear and widening fractures at the very heart of our profession that threaten to divide our entire workforce into opposing camps. Fast-track social work schemes, that take high-flying graduates from all sorts of academic backgrounds and turn them into social workers in 18 months, are facing criticism for churning out social workers at three times the cost of traditional routes (Department for Education, 2016). On the other side, graduates coming out of universities are complaining that they haven't been adequately prepared for the reality of the jobs they are going into and many also feel disadvantaged due to a lack of statutory placement experience. With bursaries being cut for traditional university students and fast-track programmes getting new awarding powers for the qualifications they provide, these divides are likely to widen.

The long-held arguments for moving social work training from a generic degree and towards specialist areas is starting to gain momentum with the news that fast-track students on the Frontline programme will no longer be able to work in adult services in Scotland or Northern Ireland. With a quarter of all new child protection social workers expected to come via such programmes by the end of the decade, that leaves a considerable number of people without the flexibility of moving to work in a different area. If such a barrier to working with a different group of people from the point of graduation onwards becomes the norm, it isn't much of a leap to decide that all students should have the option of specialising in an area that interests them most, just like our multi-agency colleagues in nursing and teaching.

Even our democratic system is fighting amongst itself when it comes to social work. Controversial plans for the Government to allow individual councils to exempt themselves from current statutory duties saw toing and froing between the two houses in the Palace of Westminster in the latter part of 2016 and early months of 2017. Plans were defeated by the Lords, then sent back to the Commons where they were reinstated again. This farcical situation only came to an end when a public petition, backed by more than 100,000 people, forced the current government to do yet another U-turn in their policies. The next looming political battle looks like it will focus on the plans to make all children's social workers go through accreditation tests. Already facing massive opposition and scaled back in scope, it is easy to imagine this being another plan to revolutionise social work that is scrapped due to it being neither wanted nor needed by those people doing the work or being supported by social workers.

Macro issues, played out on the big stages that us lowly social workers are mere observers of, eventually filter down into the meso and micro levels that we are party to. On any given evening, you can log into Facebook or look at what's happening on Twitter and see social workers arguing amongst themselves over the most trivial petty things. Somebody didn't express themselves empathetically enough to a service user in the 140 characters afforded them in a tweet. A social worker shared a meme that made fun of the fact that they are often lied to by the people they're supporting. There was a political view expressed that dared go slightly against the grain of what people in caring professions are supposed to believe in. When you see them written down like that, it becomes clear just how trivial these issues are, but look online and you will see how many social workers' lives are occupied by such meaningless arguments, often carried out in the name of 'public debate'. We end up so busy fighting amongst ourselves that we can't unite and fight for change.

Before I started blogging I used to think that the daily issues I faced were unique to my little corner of the globe and clung to the hope that there were millions of social workers all over the world who weren't facing the same issues as I was. There has to be people out there who aren't having to spend most of their working lives sat in front of computer screens writing about what they're doing when they squeeze in time with service users during unpaid overtime. There must be professionals out there who have all the resources they need and aren't having to shape their interventions based on what's available instead of what's best for the people they're supporting. Surely there are teams where social workers are settled and not wondering which of their colleagues are going to be the next ones to burn out and leave the profession forever.

I wish I could tell you that I found the promised land of social work, where person-centred practice rules the day and everything is rosy. I'd like to have been sat here writing about the fabled land of milk and honey where computers work, finance is plentiful and most of your time is spent with the people you got into this job to help in the first place. But I'm not going to lie to you. I haven't found the social work equivalent of Brigadoon in writing this book and I don't know where the best place to work is (a question I get asked a lot). Instead I have found the same frustrations manifested in slightly different ways depending on the people I have spoken to.

There's never enough money to go around and, whilst some organisations have more than others, there's always going to be a finite pot of funding that will ultimately result in some form of means-testing or financial gatekeeping.

Everyone gets annoyed by the computer recording systems that their organisations use. There are ones that are faster than others, ones that are smoother to navigate and ones that make stored documents a little bit easier to find. They all have their own frustrations and every social worker I've ever spoken to, bar none, takes issue with the amount of time they spend sat at a computer or on the telephone. Nobody goes into social work because they dream of being sat in an office for ten hours a day, we all go into it with the idealistic dream of 'helping people'. You don't dream of saving the world one case note at a time.

Then there's the stress and pressure that comes with holding such responsibility in workplaces that often make you feel like you're fighting a losing battle before you've even been out to meet someone you've just been allocated to. I interviewed almost a hundred people during the year it took me to write this book. On top of this I've interacted with hundreds of thousands of social workers from all over the world during the time I've been blogging about our profession. There isn't a single person I've ever come across who hasn't felt stressed about their job. Thankfully, most people manage to find their own personal coping mechanisms to get through their days on the frontline of social work. The healthier ones use mindfulness and exercise, the ones like me tend to eat cake and have a glass of wine most evenings after work. Those coping mechanisms sometimes wear thin and stop working for people. When that happens, the lucky ones manage to get out of their jobs or change careers before it's too late. There are others who aren't so fortunate and end up enduring such pain and pressure that they see the only escape coming from taking their own lives. I have shared the stories of some of the people who came very close to doing this in the pages of this book. However, there are others out there who weren't able to pull themselves back from the edge.

In 2012, a social worker committed suicide because her department was restructured and the pressures of her job reached unbearable levels (Cree, 2013). Speaking at the coroner's inquest

262

into her death, her husband described how his dear beloved wife "wasn't able to get through her workload without putting in extra work at home and then, with the problems with IT, her hands were tied... she wasn't able to sleep for the last five nights of her life."

More recently, in March 2016, a social worker left home to go to work at 6am and was gone for five minutes before her husband heard a knock on the family's front door. Answering the door, he found his wife lying there on the doorstep with severe burns to her body. She'd set fire to herself on a nearby patch of grass before walking back to see her husband for one last time. She died from multiple organ failure after suffering 90 percent burns to her body (Bell, 2016).

During the inquest into her death, local police commented on how a recent Ofsted inspection at work had increased the mother-of-two's stress levels. The coroner was quoted in a local newspaper as having said "she seems to have been very stressed at work after gathering accounts from people she worked with and expressed this to her husband". Her husband also spoke at the inquest and told the coroner how "she brought a lot of work home and that week she would work all the way through the night... I cannot apprehend why my brilliant wife could do this to herself and us deliberately... she loved us too much".

These two women were united by the profession they once loved so dearly, the way they doted on their families and the commitment to their jobs that saw them working above and beyond the call of duty. Tragically, they were also united by the way the jobs they had given so much of their lives to had ended up taking everything from them. Their stories should be a stark warning to all of us about what can end up happening if we are placed under too much pressure. Thinking of their husbands' words is sometimes the only thing that helps me turn off the computer and leave the office at 7pm. My reports can always be late if they have to be, but my life won't wait.

With such difficult scenes being replicated all over the world, it is little wonder that the tales finding their way between the covers of this book have ended up having a tinge of sadness to them. My goal as I set out to write this book was to capture the essence of modern social work and offer up an uncensored view of what it really means to work in this profession. If I've ended up with a collection of tales that have a maudlin tone to them, that is because the current mood within the profession is such. At the time of writing these words, a recently published study has shown that half of all social workers are looking to leave the profession within the next 18 months and most of us are working an extra ten hours for free every week (Ravalier, 2017). When you add the impact of stagnant public-sector wages, a negative media image and ongoing austerity to these findings, it's easy to see why there looks to be a creeping sense of hopelessness setting in across the entire profession.

Before you put down this book and start searching online for 'what other jobs can you do with a social work qualification' I want you to know that all is not lost. There is plenty of hope to be found out there and many committed individuals who are valiantly fighting for a better way of working.

Social workers in the Kirklees area of Yorkshire are striking for fairer working conditions and better help for the people they are supporting. Social workers from all over England have gone on a march against austerity and, in doing so, have raised awareness for the devastating impact that budget cuts are having on the most vulnerable people in our society. Social workers from

264

across Europe have been mobilising and volunteering to help Syrian refugees who have fled their war-torn country in the hope of finding sanctuary. My social work brothers and sisters in America are rallying against the politics of division that threaten to tear their country in two.

You might not find much hope coming from the governments, organisations and associations that hold the most power over our profession, but you can always find it in your fellow social workers.

Even in the saddest of tales I have set down in these pages, there is hope to be found. Where things have ended up on a sad note, there was once a happiness that proceeded the downfall. Where things have once been sad, human resilience has shone through and led to triumph. The people whose stories I have captured have shown me that, even in the most difficult of times, there is always a glimmer of hope to be found. There is always something better waiting for us out there. Sometimes we need a social worker to help us get through the tough times and sometimes we're capable of getting there ourselves.

I've spent the past decade, first as a student and then as a professional, waiting for somebody to come along and 'save' social work. From Lord Laming's reports that hoped to herald a new era of collaborative working, through to the Munro reviews that promised to reduce caseloads, streamline assessments and give social workers more time with people if they were heeded, I've seen many a false dawn in this profession.

I've heard far too many politicians offer up empty platitudes about social workers being 'unsung heroes' doing 'one of the hardest jobs', yet do nothing at all to stymie the flow of people burning out and leaving our profession because of toxic working conditions. Instead of helping their supposed 'unsung heroes', these politicians' efforts to change our profession revert to more legislation, increased scrutiny and a greater deal of pressure placed on social workers to, as David Cameron once said, 'get it right'. It's hard to 'get it right' for the people you're supporting when instead of being given more resources to do your job you're being told that it's your lack of skill that's to blame; that 'getting it right' means putting yourself through extra testing to make sure you're capable of pulling a rabbit out of a magic hat by supporting people to a higher level, but with far fewer support services in place to do so.

The experts, the politicians, the commentators in the media. Deep down they probably do believe that their bright ideas are going to 'save social work' and that opposition to their plans comes from people who are empty-headed, narrow-minded and resistant to change. But the truth is that they simply don't get what it's like to be a social worker right now. If they're an expert, their view of social work will be polarised by the data coming forth from studies that are framed by the lens of whatever research they've read most recently. If they're a civil servant, their grasp of current practice will be shaped by the information that councils offer up to them during their high-level meetings and stage-managed visits to hastily tidied offices. If they're a politician, their vision of what social work should entail will be moulded by the political ideologies that led them into their parties in the first place (save for people like Emma Lewell-Buck, whose story is in Chapter Three, who was a social worker before she became an MP).

These people whose words and actions shape our practice don't know what it's like to do our jobs. They don't know what it's like when you're a newly qualified social worker with 46 allocated cases and being told that it's 'sink or swim' in frontline child protection. 46 children to care for who have all experienced some form of abuse or neglect in their lives, often going back many years.

46 children with two parents that you must work with, empower, support and encourage to help keep their little ones' safe. 46 children with stepdads, stepmums and parents' boyfriends or girlfriends that you have to work with too. Parents and partners who often have significant criminal histories, mental health concerns, substance misuse issues or who are perpetrators of domestic abuse.

Most of the time people won't want you in their lives. Sometimes they will threaten you. Occasionally you will be abused and assaulted for simply doing your job.

As well as the children and their parents, you've got to keep in touch with all the professionals that are connected to the children and their carers as well. Teachers, health visitors, midwives, support workers, probation officers, community nurses, drug and alcohol workers, housing officers, nursery nurses and lots more people all to work in partnership with.

Those in power don't seem to understand that you have to write down everything you do for each of those 46 children, their parents and hundreds of professionals. Every phone call, every visit, every meeting, every passing conversation, they all have to be 'recorded or it didn't happen'.

For each of those 46 children there are deadlines you must meet. A visit every fortnight, a meeting every four weeks, a review every three months. All those visits, meetings and reviews have to be typed up within 48 hours of them happening as well.

There's a procedure that you have to follow for every one of those visits, meetings and reviews, but this will often change depending on who you ask. There's a template for every report and recording, but these will often be ripped up and rewritten at the whim of a new senior manager. There's a process for how you're meant to work, but this is often disconnected from the reality you face every single day and is dreamed up by people who've forgotten what it's like to be in your shoes.

There's no acknowledgment that you're given the responsibility for keeping those 46 children safer than they've even been before, but getting all of the things that used to help you do this taken away from you.

The children's centres have closed down. The domestic violence awareness courses are no longer running. The women's refuge has run out of funding. Parenting programmes are now reserved for the parents whose children are in care. The youth workers have all been sacked. You've lost your social work assistants and admin staff.

You wonder if you're allowed to do this work yourself because, after all, you came into this job to 'help people'. But the reports won't write themselves and the visits need typing up straight away or your name will be highlighted in red when the weekly performance figures go out.

You end up spending 80% of your time on the computer writing about what you'd like to do, but only 20% of your time out there seeing the children you're asked to protect. When you eventually see the children and their parents, you're often making excuses for why services aren't there anymore and explaining away delays in them getting the help they really need.

You're paid for 37 hours a week to do all of this, but you most often do more than 50.

Every month there's somebody leaving your office and you never know how long the next face through the door is going to last before they also up and leave. When you look for hope that things are going to get better, that somebody is offering an answer to the issues you're facing, you find nothing.

You find a government that changes the minister responsible for looking after your profession every year. Then, when they do have a plan to make things better, it simply involves more paperwork and more blame put onto you and your colleagues. You find a professional association ran by people who haven't done your job for years and spend most of their time talking about what they'd like to do, but very little time spent changing things at all. You find a regulator that appears to take boundless joy in punishing your fellow professionals for being the victims of abuse, speaking out about their jobs online and striking off workers who have been broken by toxic workplaces. You find a management culture that thrives on bullying and you soon learn the only way to survive is by keeping your head down and never complaining. You find a media that paints your profession like child snatchers and blames you for the death of children that are killed by their own parents.

Despite all of these issues, you're desperate to do your best to help people. So you take the blame for everything. You're the face of your department, the face of your council, the face of your profession and the face of your government. The people you work with can't complain to those in power who shape their lives, but they can complain to you. That sees you taking the flak for everything and ending up as part of the same broken system that you know is failing the very people you want to help.

But remember that, amongst all of this, you've still got those 46 children to look after...

A third professional regulator in six years isn't going to magically reduce the demand on social services that is driven by intergenerational neglect which has been decades in the making. Fast-tracked and high-flying students are still going to end up working in the same toxic workplaces that will eventually end up grinding them down, no matter how skilled they are in systemic practice. Accreditation tests aren't going to bring back the youth clubs, community centres and support services that provided the early intervention which prevented people needing targeted social services support in the first place. No amount of innovation is going to make a difference when hospitals are overflowing and you can't even find a bed for your patient within a hundred miles of their home.

Basic business sense dictates that organisations live and die by listening to two sets of people, those who use their services and those who are on the shop floor. This model appears to be upside down in contemporary public services, with the voices of those doing the work and benefitting from the work being wholly marginalised. Instead of hearing from the two sets of people that matter the most, and shaping our profession to their needs, we are instead lectured to from up on high by people who have either never been a social worker, or have all but forgotten what it feels like to work 50 hours a week in a professional position yet still worry if you've got enough money left over at the end of the month to put fuel in your car.

You might not find much hope coming from the governments, organisations and associations that hold the most power over our profession, but you can always find it in your fellow social workers. That is the message I want to leave you with.

Look to your colleague who works late every day yet still finds the time to volunteer with the Samaritans and go on political marches. Look to the teenage student on placement who, despite all the negative news stories she has read about social work failings, still wants to dedicate her working life to the service of others. Look to your manager who refuses to let the performance indicator culture of his seniors dictate his supervision and always finds time to see the person behind the paperwork. Look to yourself and ask what you can do to help make your profession better for all of us.

When you get past the rules, guidance and legislation that shapes our practice and move beyond the social work cycle of assessment, intervention and review that provides a metronomic flow to our duties year after year, you find that our profession is based on hope. The hope that things will get better, the hope that we can make a difference, the hope that people are capable of moving on from past mistakes. If we didn't believe in hope, we wouldn't have become social workers in the first place. Every aspect of our profession is rooted in the hope that people are capable of achieving anything, just so long as they have a helping hand along the way.

Martin Luther King Jr. once said "we must accept finite disappointment, but never lose infinite hope" and I can't help but thinking his words are a fitting mantra for what we face in modern social work. We're never going to catch up on our recording, we'll never get that 'to do' list completed and there will always be a deadline just around the corner. Some people will never want us in their lives and sometimes, no matter how hard we work, we'll never make the breakthrough people need. But we can't lose hope that we're making a difference in the world and we can't lose hope that we are capable of so much more than we're showing right now.

Keep hoping. Keep trying. Keep social working.

References

Bell, G (2016) 'Essex social worker told 999 she had set herself on fire'. *Essex Live*. [Online] Available at: http://www.essexlive.news/essex-mother-husband-severe-burns-death/story-29342706-detail/story.html [Accessed: 24th August 2017]

Brindle, D & Carvel, J (2008) 'We said never again after *Climbié*. We were wrong'. *The Guardian*. 12th November 2008

Butler-Sloss, E (1988) *Report of the inquiry into child abuse in Cleveland* 1987. London: Her Majesty's Stationery Office

Cafcass (2017) Care *applications* [Online] Available at: https://www.cafcass.gov.uk/leaflets-resources/organisational-material/care-and-private-law-demand-statistics/care-demand-statistics.aspx [Accessed: 24th August 2017]

Campbell, B (1997) *Unofficial Secrets: Child Abuse - The Cleveland Case.* London: Virago

Children's Commissioner (2017) *Stability Index: Overview and Initial Findings* [Online] Available at: https://www.childrenscommissioner.gov.uk/wp-content/uploads/2017/06/Childrens-Commissioners-Stability-Index-2017-Overview-Document-1.3.pdf [Accessed: 24th August 2017]

Coran Voice (2015) *Children and Young People's Views on Being in Care* [Online] Available at: http://cdn.basw.co.uk/upload/basw_32034-9.pdf [Accessed: 24th August 2017]

Cree, J (2013) 'Job drove Clitheroe social worker to suicide'. *The Lancashire Telegraph*. 7th February 2013

Department for Education (2016) Comparing the costs of social work qualification routes. [Online] Available at: https://www.gov.uk/government/uploads/system/uploads/attachment_data/file/510361/DFE-RR517-Social-work-qualification-routes-comparing_the_costs.pdf [Accessed: 24th August 2017]

Department for Work and Pensions (2017) Households Below Average Income: An analysis of the UK income distribution: 1994/95-2015/16 [Online] Available at: https://www.gov.uk/government/uploads/system/uploads/attachment_data/file/600091/households-below-average-income-1994-1995-2015-2016.pdf [Accessed: 24th August 2017]

Donovan, T (2011) 'Profile: Sharon Shoesmith', BBC News. 27th May 2011 [Online] Available at: http://news.bbc.co.uk/local/london/hi/tv_and_radio/newsid_8639000/8639697.stm [Accessed: 24th August 2017]

Fallon, D & Broadhurst, K (2016) Preventing Unplanned Pregnancy and Improving Preparation for Parenthood for Care-Experienced Young People. London: Coram

Glover, V (2016) 'Maternal Anxiety, Depression, and Stress During Pregnancy: Effects on the Fetus and the Child, and Underlying

Mechanisms'. Fetal Development

213-227. 10.1007/978-3-319-22023-9

Haringey Council (2005) Provisional attainment data for Key Stages 1-4, GCE A Level and attendance including children Looked After by the Council [Online] Available at: https://minutes.haringey.gov.uk/Data/Children's%20Service%20Advisory%20Committee/20051017/Agenda/$Item%2010%20Provisional%20Attainment%20Data.doc.pdf [Accessed: 24th August 2017]

HM Government (2006) Working together to safeguard children: a guide to interagency working to safeguard and promote the welfare of children. London: The Stationery Office

Home Office (2008) Home Office Statistical Bulletin: Homicides, Firearm Offences and Intimate Violence 2007/08 [Online] Available at: http://webarchive.nationalarchives.gov.uk/20110220110338/ http://rds.homeoffice.gov.uk/rds/pdfs09/hosb0209.pdf [Accessed: 24th August 2017]

House of Commons Health Committee (2003) The Victoria Climbié

Inquiry Report: Sixth Report of Session 2002–03 [Online] Available at: https://publications.parliament.uk/pa/cm200203/cmselect/cmhealth/570/570.pdf [Accessed: 24th August 2017]

McNicoll, A (2017) 'Frontline graduates face restrictions on practising outside of England'. Community Care. April 3rd 2017

Morris, N (2009) 'Shocking sickness rates in social work' The Independent. 15th September 2009

Munro, E (2011) The Munro review of child protection: final report – a child-centred system. London: Department for Education

Office for National Statistics (2016) Domestic abuse in England and Wales: year ending March 2016 [Online] Available at: https://www.ons.gov.uk/peoplepopulationandcommunity/crimeandjustice/bulletins/domesticabuseinenglandandwales/yearendingmarch2016 [Accessed: 24th August 2017]

Ofsted (2008) The Annual Report of Her Majesty's Chief Inspector of Education, Children's Services and Skills 2007/08 Norwich: The Stationery Office

O'Hara, M (2009) 'Glasvegas get lyrical about social work'. The Guardian. 11th March 2009

Parton, N (2014) The Politics of Child Protection: Contemporary Developments and Future Directions London: Palgrave

Prison Reform Trust (2017) In Care, Out of Trouble: Impact report. [Online] Available at: http://www.prisonreformtrust.org.uk/Portals/0/Documents/Care%20review%20impact%20report%20Jan%202017%20UPDATE%20FINAL.pdf [Accessed: 24th August 2017]

Ravalier, J (2017) UK Social Workers: Working Conditions and Wellbeing. Bath: Bath Spa University and BASW

The Guardian (2009) The blame game: how death of a toddler led to dismissal [Online] Available at: https://www.theguardian.com/society/2009/feb/06/baby-p-haringey-childrens-ministry [Accessed: 24th August 2017]

University of Bedfordshire (2013) Social workers 'life expectancy' just eight years [Online] Available at: https://www.beds.ac.uk/news/2013/january/social-workers-life-expectancy-just-eight-years [Accessed: 24th August 2017]

Wainwright, D (2016) England children's social worker posts almost 20% vacant. BBC News 20th April 2016 [Online] Available at: http://www.bbc.co.uk/news/uk-england-36026098 [Accessed: 24th August 2017]

Women's Aid (2017) The Femicide Census 2017 [Online] Available at: https://www.womensaid.org.uk/what-we-do/campaigning-and-influencing/femicide-census [Accessed: 24th August 2017]

Manufactured by Amazon.ca
Bolton, ON

10297774R00153